SURVIVING
MEDICINE

THE MED SCHOOL YEARS

To my wife, Charlotte, who convinced me to do this

I began drawing cartoons at medical school as a light-hearted way to portray the ridiculous world of medicine; its excitement, fulfilment and anxiety, and how it feels to be thrown right into the middle of it all. I had also gradually been putting together a blog of useful tips and tricks for medical students that I had picked up along the way, and the two projects remained distinct, until some bright spark (my wife) suggested the two would work well together. What I hoped to create was an easy, memorable and entertaining way to learn useful little bits of medical advice without 'studying'. I found I would frequently want to read something that wasn't 'work' but was still useful for my learning, and that is the niche this book aims to fill. Some of the cartoons have a specific intended learning point, others are entirely ridiculous and serve only to entertain.

As for the name 'unicyclemedic' – I was given my first unicycle as a birthday present and immediately fell in love with the challenge of mastering a very difficult and completely pointless new skill. I found that time spent riding a unicycle was time well spent, therapeutic even. It forces you to clear your head and concentrate on the task at hand, because the minute your mind starts to wander, to worry and fret about work, you fall off. I found it to be the perfect complement to a stressful life learning to be a doctor, and would thoroughly recommend it to anyone.

I hope you enjoy reading this book as much as I enjoyed putting it together, and implore you to make time for the pointless fun in life.

unicyclemedic.com
@unicyclemedic
@unicycle_medic

SURVIVING
MEDICINE

THE MED SCHOOL YEARS

WILL SLOPER

MBBS, MA (Cantab.)

Scion

ISBN 9781911510253

First published 2018

Scion Publishing Limited

The Old Hayloft, Vantage Business Park, Bloxham Road, Banbury OX16 9UX, UK
www.scionpublishing.com

Important Note from the Publisher

The information contained within this book was obtained by Scion Publishing Ltd from sources believed by us to be reliable. However, while every effort has been made to ensure its accuracy, no responsibility for loss or injury whatsoever occasioned to any person acting or refraining from action as a result of information contained herein can be accepted by the authors or publishers.

Although every effort has been made to ensure that all owners of copyright material have been acknowledged in this publication, we would be pleased to acknowledge in subsequent reprints or editions any omissions brought to our attention.

Registered names, trademarks, etc. used in this book, even when not marked as such, are not to be considered unprotected by law.

Typeset by Medlar Publishing Solutions Pvt Ltd, India
Printed and bound in Great Britain by Severn, Gloucester

Last digit is the print number: 10 9 8 7 6 5 4 3 2 1

Contents

Preface

Welcome to the family, and congratulations on joining us on our delectably haphazard journey through the perplexing world of medicine. From dozing wearily through frankly excessive first year anatomy lectures to venturing out into the wilderness of the wards and beyond, we've all been exactly where you are right now, and we all remember how it felt – exhilarating, terrifying, overwhelming, inspiring. Few careers exist with such a personal level of shared experience between colleagues of all ages, and that's the reason I decided to put this book together. As you walk wide-eyed in anticipation through the creaking doors of your prestigious new medical school, you'll most likely get slapped in the face with an enormous reading list of dishearteningly thick 'recommended' textbooks that will teach you the incredibly diverse and detailed theory of medicine and surgery, how to perform examinations and procedures in a safe and effective manner, and reams of drugs that I promise you even the veteran pharmacists haven't memorised.

But what you don't get given is someone to reassure you when you think you can't do it, to pat you on the back when you finally understand something that everyone else seemed to grasp effortlessly, or a solution to all the frankly insane situations that arise on the ward, like when you can't find a vein on an elderly patient or an intoxicated intravenous drug user starts throwing faeces at the nursing staff.

In all honesty, medicine is such a vast and unpredictable beast that you simply cannot attempt to prepare for *every* situation, so instead I hope this helps to prepare you for *any* situation; to aid you as you build your own personal toolkit of techniques, tricks and tips to ensure that whatever happens, you can at least do *something*.

And remember, you are *never* alone.

Will Sloper
Unicyclemedic
July 2018

CHAPTER ONE:

Airway, Breathing, Circulation

Airway

The first time I opened the airway of an unresponsive patient at medical school, the ensuing life-restoring breath that was allowed to escape from their creaking lungs was so pungent that I instantly threw up in my mouth, and only just managed to slam my own jaw shut in time to stop it landing right in the airway I had just opened.

ABC BY SPECIALTY

ANAESTHETICS   MEDICAL

AIRWAY   ARRIVE
BAGEL   BERATE
COFFEE   CRITICISE
                      DEPART

CARDIOLOGY   ORTHO

ADMIT TO ACU   ARRIVE
BETA BLOCKER   BONES!?
CARDIOVERT   COOL.
DIGOXIN
EXPLAIN HANDWRITING

DERMATOLOGY

AWAY → LEAVE MESSAGE
BACK → PATIENT STILL HERE?
COAT IN STEROIDS
                    unreadable

If you take just one thing away from your time at medical school then it's quite likely you'll fail because there's a lot of important stuff to learn. But probably the single most important thing to remember is this:

If there's air going in and out, and blood going round and round, you've got at least a couple of minutes to get some senior help.

If there isn't air going in and out, then you have a couple of minutes before the lack of effective circulation does any sort of permanent damage – you have a lot more time than you think – so take a deep breath, and start your ABCs.

The slickest way I've found to open an airway is to slide your non-dominant hand under the back of their head towards their neck as if scooping up a basketball. With the other hand you can point gleefully at your impeccable technique. Or you can do something useful like lifting their chin and having a look (from an angle) to see if there's anything in their mouth obstructing the airway. If you see something, grab some forceps and go fishing. Don't put your hand inside someone's mouth because:

1. It's gross

2. If they have a seizure they'll bite your fingers off.

The infamous jawthrust is good because it really works. It also really hurts, so you can simultaneously open their airway and assess their response to pain if they're unresponsive. From the front, hook your fingers around the angle of the jaw and press hard on the cheekbones with your thumbs. If they scream, *voilà!* they're breathing, their airway is open, and they're perfusing their brain enough to shout.

Well done you.

Pro tip:

Attempting to jawthrust a conscious patient is unlikely to be of benefit to anyone.

Breathing

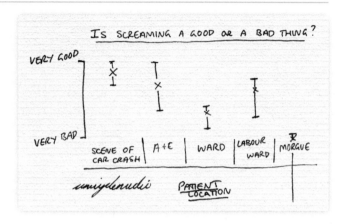

Location, location, location

Screaming is rarely good, but in the context of an ABC assessment it can be quite helpful, as it tells you immediately that the patient has a clear airway, is breathing enough to make a noise and is perfusing their brain enough to turn that noise into a scream. If they're not screaming, and you're happy their airway is clear, then the things to check in breathing include:

▶ Is the chest wall moving equally on both sides?

▶ Is there significant respiratory distress? (tracheal tug, intercostal recession)

▶ What are their oxygen saturations?

▶ Is air reaching the bases of the lungs? (auscultation)

If their saturations are poor or they're demonstrating significant signs of respiratory distress, then pop 15L oxygen on through a non-rebreathe mask, and go back to airway and start again. If all of the above are fine, you can probably move on to circulation.

Circulation

Once you're happy that oxygen is reaching the blood through the airway and lungs, the next task is to determine whether that oxygen is reaching the tissues. There are a number of ways of measuring this:

▶ If there's blood all over the floor, then it's not doing its job inside the body. This sounds obvious, but you have to *actively look* for signs of bleeding.

Pro tip:
The one time that you don't start with airway in your assessment is in the case of catastrophic haemorrhage, such as a traumatically amputated limb with a huge arterial bleed. In this case you should control the bleeding first with a tourniquet, then continue with airway assessment.

▶ Blood pressure tells you how well the heart is pumping. The systolic number should ideally be above at least 90mmHg to perfuse the brain adequately.

Pro tip:
Look at the difference between the systolic and diastolic numbers. 130/45 is a 'wide' pulse pressure, while 90/75 is considered 'narrow'. A wide pulse pressure suggests the resistance of the vasculature is low, as seen in vasodilated states such as sepsis. A narrow pulse pressure may highlight a vasoconstricted state such as blood loss, as the blood vessels squeeze shut to preserve blood volume.

▶ Pulse gives an idea of how hard the heart is having to work (it'll be pumping much faster if the patient has lost a lot of blood).

▶ Capillary refill time shows how well they are perfusing their extremities. If you squeeze their finger until it goes pale, and it takes less than 2 seconds to return to normal colour, they're doing all right. If it takes longer, or it is already pale, then press on their sternum for a 'central' capillary refill. If the refill time for the sternum is quicker than the finger, then they're moderately 'shut down'. If both refill times are slow, then they're very shut down indeed. At this point it might be wise to consider popping in a big cannula or two and giving some fluid, or blood products if you suspect a lot of bleeding.

Everything you need to know about bleeding

Bleeding is scary. Torrential haemorrhage is terrifying. I've only seen one person die from blood loss and honestly I couldn't understand how so much blood came out of such a small person. The sound of it hitting the floor was particularly unforgettable. The key with bleeding is acting quickly, and doing as many sensible things as you can, so here are my sensible things to do when a patient is bleeding big time.

▶ You can bleed your entire circulating volume into five places; chest, abdomen, pelvis, a long bone fracture and onto the floor. Make sure you've determined where the blood is going.

▶ If there's huge bleeding from a limb, a tourniquet buys you lots of time. The tourniquet should hurt almost as badly as the wound itself. Only put tourniquets over limb sections with one long bone (thigh or upper arm), and please don't tourniquet the neck. If possible lift the bleeding area above the level of the heart.

▶ You have about five litres of blood to play with in a normal sized person – what comes out, should probably go back in. This means they need big cannulas wherever you can get them in. Don't be scared of intraosseous access if it's needed.

▶ All patients with bleeding need a full blood count to help quantify what they've lost, and a crossmatch so that they can be transfused (*if they're willing to be transfused, that is – a whole other kettle of bleeding fish*).

▶ Urine output will tell you if there's enough blood to perfuse the kidneys, consciousness will let you know if they're perfusing their brain. If either are getting worse, the bleeding hasn't stopped.

▶ If they're vomiting blood, they need endoscopy as soon as possible, so make sure they've got two big cannulae in and contact the gastroenterologist on call.

▶ The best thing to replace blood is blood. Litres of fluid will initially help blood pressure but not oxygenation of the tissues.

Pro tip:

One way or another, all bleeding stops eventually.

▶ Tranexamic acid and vitamin K are great for dealing with persistent bleeds, especially if warfarin is involved. If all else fails, Beriplex or Octaplex will bring an INR down from 4 to 1 in minutes if life-threatening bleeding is resistant to other measures.

Disability

Once you have assessed and managed airway, breathing and circulation, you have a 'haemodynamically stable' patient, and can move onto D – disability. This is where you assess the neurological status of the patient to ensure their brain isn't compromised.

Coning is herniation of the cerebellar tonsils through the foramen magnum, possibly causing Cushing's triad of bradycardia, hypertension and erratic respiration. It is a very late sign of increased intracranial pressure, and you don't really want to get to that point before calling for help as there's not a whole lot that can be done once you get to this point. Other indicators include unequal pupils, nausea and vomiting, headache worse on lying down and altered consciousness. Papilloedema is also a late sign.

The things to assess in disability are:

▶ Glasgow Coma Scale (GCS), a measure of alertness from 3 to 15 with three categories:

Eyes	4 – open spontaneously
	3 – open to voice
	2 – open to pain
	1 – no response
Verbal	5 – talking sensibly
	4 – confused
	3 – words, not making sense
	2 – noises, no words
	1 – no response
Motor	6 – follows commands
	5 – localises to pain
	4 – withdraws from pain
	3 – abnormally flexes to pain
	2 – abnormally extends to pain
	1 – no response

A simpler version is AVPU (are they **a**lert, responding to **v**oice, **p**ain or **u**nresponsive?). GCS is important because if they score below 8, then there is a risk their airway reflexes will fail and they won't maintain their own airway, even if it is open at the moment.

Once you have measured their GCS, the key is to document it, and keep reassessing regularly to see if there is a change that might suggest clinical improvement (if increasing) or something bad like increasing intracranial pressure (if decreasing).

▶ Pupils – are their pupils equal and reactive to light? If their pupils are unequal, something is probably squashing one of the oculomotor or optic nerves. If they are pinpoint small, think of opiate overdose, and if they're sluggish or very dilated then consider other drug toxicity.

Pro tip:

'Below eight, intubate' – consider airway adjuncts or intubation if their GCS is below 8.

Pro tip:

DEFG – Don't ever forget glucose. Someone may be unconscious because their blood glucose is too low. A quick fingertip test can tell you a lot of information!

Exposure

Last but not least in the primary survey is exposure. This is your final check to make sure you haven't missed anything, and involves inspecting your patient from head to toe to look for injuries, bleeding, rashes and pain that you may have missed earlier.

Pro tip:

Be sure to pull the bedsheets down to inspect the groin and back properly. A common simulation (and real-life) case is a patient with slightly low blood pressure who seems quite well, and only upon pulling back the sheets do you notice a huge rectal bleed.

Once you have examined your patient for injuries and felt their abdomen for lumps, bumps and tenderness (and made sure you're not missing any burns!), you can go back and reassess once again, starting with A, B, C…

CHAPTER TWO:

Histories

I honestly thought I was fairly well prepared for my first attempt at taking a history from a real live patient. I had read the instructions on how to structure a history:

▶ Presenting complaint – *why are they here?*

▶ History of presenting complaint – *what led up to them coming in?*

▶ Previous medical history – *if it happened before it'll probably happen again*

▶ Allergies, alcohol, smoking, drugs, medications

▶ Social history – *do they live alone? What job do they do?*

▶ Family history – *anyone else with the same issue?*

▶ Review of systems – *can I find anything I've missed?*

So in I walked, primed and ready to whip out a sneaky respiratory, cardiac or neurological diagnosis, and confidently introduced myself to the lady in front of me, and began what was to be my first, and worst ever clerking.

"May I ask – what was the reason that you came to hospital?"

Silence.

The haggard, grey, glassy-eyed lady of 72 that sat before me stared blankly through the back of my head, blinking uncomfortably infrequently, her rattling breath oddly hypnotic. I started to sweat.

"Are you all right?"

The silence continued for what seemed like more than a minute, until finally, knifing through the palpable tension, a golden sliver of pearlescent sputum meekly made its presence known and began its majestic descent from her hanging mouth, abseiling down to nestle gently on the back of the white-knuckled fist that clung relentlessly to what I assume was previously a non-bent spoon.

"Well, thank you very much, I'll leave you to it."

Pro tip: 💡

Don't take your first ever history from a heavily medicated psychiatric patient.

I called it a day and went home to have a think about whether I was really all that cut out for this job.

The presenting complaint is the first part of every history. It is the title of the problem, and guides the rest of the history as you dig deeper into the patient's story. The presenting complaint should be the problem *in the patient's own words*. 'Short of breath', 'Chest pain' and 'Tiredness' are presenting complaints. 'Jaundice', 'Cardiac pain' and 'Peritonism' are clinical assessments. (Although to be completely fair, I did have a patient who said in his own words that he was having 'an atypical infective exacerbation of COPD', because he was a retired GP who had diagnosed himself and was trying to speed the process along.)

The pinnacle of medicine is making that diagnosis, and as a wizened consultant once advised me, 85% of diagnoses are made from the history alone. Finding the correct diagnosis is finding the key that unlocks the door in front of you and allows you to treat the disabling condition that has, until now, cursed the poor soul before you. Let the patient be your guide. Searching for the diagnosis is like trying to find a certain room in a large building complex. The quickest and easiest way to find the right room is to ask the person who knows where the rooms are and who has all the keys.

This person is the patient.

Ask them where to go, and let them lead you. Don't try and jump ahead, just follow them to the correct destination. If you start jumping, thinking 'I bet this is pneumonia', you're essentially running ahead to a random room and asking 'is it in here?'. Wait until the patient has told you everything, and see where you've ended up. You'll be amazed at how much a patient will reveal when given a minute to speak after being asked,

"What seems to be the problem?"

Socrates

After ABC, Socrates is possibly the most commonly used acronym in the world of medicine, certainly in med school, and for good reason. It provides a reliable backbone of the patient's presenting complaint, particularly when it comes to pain, upon which you can begin to build the flesh of an adequate clinical history.

If you do nothing else, just make sure you have at least Socrates-ed your patient's symptoms. All of them – pain, bloating, itching, rashes – the lot. Don't fret about what the overarching diagnosis might be, or how the symptoms are supposed to fit together, just ask the questions, and then write the responses down. Soon you'll find yourself looking at a page of useful information that begins to tell you (or more likely your consultant) the correct diagnosis. It's not about finding the answer at this stage, it's about harvesting enough useful information.

Site

Where is the pain? A logical first question that gets the ball rolling and guides you to where the pathology is likely to be. Sometimes it will be a more obvious question than others, but when someone comes in with abdominal pain, it matters a lot whether it started in the right upper quadrant:

▶ Liver

▶ Lung (*posteriorly the lung is right down in the upper abdomen*)

▶ Gall bladder

▶ Pancreas (*technically central and left but often felt on the right*)

Or left lower quadrant:

▶ Colon

▶ Ovary

▶ Bladder

▶ Hernias

Pro tip: 💡

Courvoisier's law states that painless jaundice with a palpable gall bladder is most likely not caused by gallstones.

Onset

The onset of pain can tell you a lot about what's causing it, if you understand the pathophysiology that's at play. I tend to divide it into three:

▸ Sudden

▸ Quick

▸ Gradual.

As a general rule, if a pain comes on very suddenly, something has:

▶ Burst

▶ Blocked, or

▶ Broken.

This can represent a blood vessel tearing, as in aortic dissection or aneurysm rupture, perforation of the gut in diverticulosis or a duodenal ulcer, or damage to a viscus (often the spleen) following significant trauma. 'Blocked' usually represents embolism, where something breaks off and gets stuck elsewhere, such as a portion of atherosclerotic plaque in the leg breaking off and getting lodged in the lungs. It can also be caused by the gradual build-up of plaque or thrombus that has finally reached that critical point where there is no longer sufficient blood flow to supply the organ in question, as is often seen in myocardial infarction.

Very gradual pain that has built over months or years is more suggestive of something that is:

▶ Growing, such as a tumour, or

▶ Grinding down, as in osteoarthritis of the knees or spine.

Pain that comes on quickly can be caused by a wide array of pathologies, from inflammation to bleeding, so you need to corroborate it with other aspects of the history to figure it out.

Pro tip: 💡

If someone has unrelenting bone pain at night that wakes them from sleep, it's malignancy until proven otherwise.

Character

What the pain feels like can reveal what type of pathology is at play. The shooting pain of impinged nerve routes, the burning sting of oesophageal reflux and the relentless crushing of cardiac ischaemia are all commonly described by patients with impressive accuracy. Don't load the question by saying *"Is it a burning pain?"*; ask how they would describe it, and if they can't think of anything, then you can suggest *'burning, cramping, stinging, shooting…'*

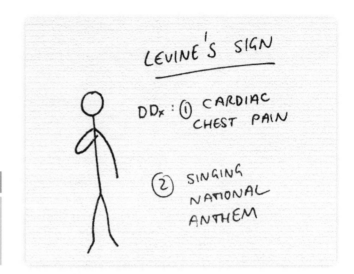

Radiation

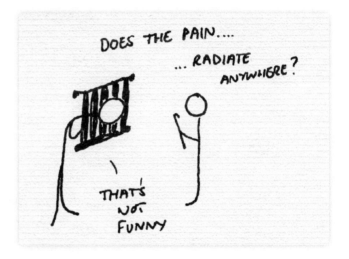

Loin pain radiating to the groin suggests kidney or ureter pathology, cardiac chest pain typically radiates down the arm and to the jaw, and shoulder tip pain can suggest irritation of the diaphragm as the C3 dermatome gets triggered via the phrenic nerve.

Referred pain occurs when pain signals from a sparsely innervated viscus travel along similar pathways to those originating from much more densely innervated structures such as skin and muscle. Your brain receives the signals and assumes they came from the statistically more likely source, so you 'feel' diaphragm pain in your shoulder.

> **Pro tip:** 💡
>
> *Sod's law states that the more a person's pain sounds like textbook cardiac chest pain, complete with radiation to the jaw and left arm, the less likely it is to actually be cardiac in origin. Equally, the elderly and those with diabetes or who are on steroids can present with 'silent' myocardial infarction, with no pain at all. You know, just to make things difficult.*

Associated symptoms

What else is going on? Are they vomiting, having diarrhoea or maybe even bleeding? Have they noticed any other symptoms that coincide with the main reason they've come in?

AND THIS DISCHARGE, DID IT DISSOLVE THROUGH THE FLOOR OR JUST SIT THERE?

OH GOD NO IT JUST STAYED THERE

I LIKE TO REASSURE ANXIOUS PATIENTS BY ASKING STRANGE QUESTIONS, TO SHOW HOW BAD IT COULD BE.

Often you have to reverse this question, as patients will come in reporting a whole array of symptoms and you won't know where to start. A good question to ask is, *"Which symptom is troubling you most?"* as this will give you your presenting complaint, around which you can then start to construct the rest of the history.

Timing

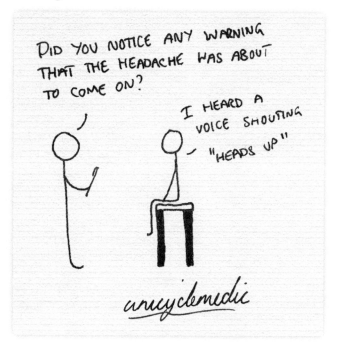

DID YOU NOTICE ANY WARNING THAT THE HEADACHE WAS ABOUT TO COME ON?

I HEARD A VOICE SHOUTING "HEADS UP"

A good question to ask, but not always helpful

Is it worse in the morning when they wake up or at the end of the day? Pain that is there after a day of moving around suggests a 'wear and tear' type of picture such as osteoarthritis, usually of the knee or spine. Inflammatory pain such as rheumatoid arthritis, on the other hand, tends to be worse after long periods of staying still, so patients say they wake up feeling very stiff and sore, but it gradually loosens over the course of the day. Likewise, a headache that is worse in the morning but improves after a period of standing may hint at raised intracranial pressure. Chest pain twenty minutes after a meal can be a heart attack, but chest pain twenty minutes after *every* meal is almost certainly reflux.

Exacerbating and relieving factors

Have they found anything that makes it better or worse? Often the answer is no, or paracetamol, but sometimes they'll give you little clues, such as leaning forward in pericarditis or the rigid stillness of a peritonitic abdomen. Arterial insufficiency pain is generally better when they hang their foot out of the bed, while venous insufficiency

Pro tip: 💡

Patients with arterial insufficiency to the legs will often rub their thighs as if 'massaging' the blood down to the feet.

pain is better when the leg is elevated above the level of the hips.

Severity out of ten

Asking a patient how bad their pain is will tell you several things. Firstly, how severe it is, and whether they need more pain relief. Secondly, it can hint towards the pathology at hand – a perforated bowel causing peritonitis is unlikely to be a 2/10. Thirdly, it allows you to see how their pain is changing. A person who can eloquently describe exactly how awful their excruciating, enveloping, overwhelming, stabbing pain is, is probably in less pain than the person not speaking because they're concentrating so hard on just breathing. Having said that, pain is a very personal experience, so don't jump to assume that someone's pain isn't what they say it is!

Pro tip:

If a young person has worsening limb pain despite lots of morphine, you need to start thinking about compartment syndrome (see the section on Orthopaedics in Chapter 3).

Drugs and stuff

Aim high. If you ask someone who takes illicit drugs whether they take illicit drugs, they're going to confidently respond with a resounding 'No' because you're not supposed to take illicit drugs and no one in their right mind is going to confess to the question when other people might be listening. If, however, you calmly ask:

"Any cocaine, heroin, or ketamine?" as if it's as normal as coffee or chocolate, they're much more likely to be honest and say, *"Oh Lord no, just a bit of cannabis."*

The same applies to smoking. Asking 'how much do you smoke?' will likely receive somewhat of an 'underestimate', because people know they're not supposed to smoke and don't want to say something that then makes their doctor recoil in horror. Start with a very high suggestion and you'll get something closer to the truth.

Pro tip: 💡

Try not to recoil in horror. Be it upon hearing of a particularly vigorous alcohol regime or pulling back the sheets to find toenails touching the kneecaps, at least try to maintain an air of calm. No patient wants to think they're the 'worst you've ever seen', even if they really are.

"Ten packs a day?"

"Absolutely not. Four at a push."

Allergies

Always, always, always ask about allergies. It cannot be stressed how important it is to know what the patient's body will absolutely not tolerate. Missing other stuff is fine, you can ask again later, but make sure you walk away from the patient knowing whether or not that antibiotic you plan to prescribe is going to do a lot more harm than good.

Very few people will deny allergies that they actually have, but many people will claim that they are allergic to a drug when actually it's a known side effect or caused by something else entirely, so specifically ask *what happens* if they take that drug, touch that metal, or eat 'just the blue Skittles'. If they get short of breath, wheezy, start swelling up like a balloon or get a very itchy rash, then it's a true allergy. Feeling mildly nauseous after Snickers number five is called a 'survival mechanism'.

Pro tip:

Once you've done your history, remember to take a trip to **ASDA** (Alcohol, Smoking, Drugs, Allergies).

Pro tip:

If their fingernails are tar stained all the way up to the nail bed, they haven't given up smoking. If there is a band of clean nail poking out from a stained finger, then they may well have kicked the habit recently – an achievement not to be sniffed at.

Sometimes the unmistakable odour of a seventy pack-year history will present itself as an almost palpable cloud of smoke surrounding a somewhat short of breath patient. Look at the fingernails and you'll see that familiar tar staining.

Regular medications

The 'pharmagroan' is the noise the clerking doctor makes when they see just how many medications the 94-year-old patient in front of them is taking. I promise you will learn your own pharmagroan in good time.

Most patients in hospital nowadays are on multiple medications – 'polypharmacy'. Like it or loathe it, the western healthcare system loves to jump in with a nice and convenient 'pill for every ill', and as a result the majority of hospital visits result in a very frustrating twenty minutes of working out exactly what medications a patient is taking, whether they *are actually taking them (very important to ask)*, and why. One thing to remember is that their list can tell you a lot about the other health conditions they forgot to tell you about when you asked them what health conditions they have. They may say they have a 'bit of blood pressure', but if they're on ramipril, amlodipine, bumetanide and bisoprolol, they probably have a *lot* of blood pressure, that their poor GP has spent years trying to get under control.

If they're on anything ending in '-mab' they've got a lot of inflammation going on somewhere, likely an autoimmune condition such as rheumatoid arthritis. If you can see from previous admissions that they've routinely needed Pabrinex and chlordiazepoxide as an inpatient, then that 'one glass of wine a day' isn't quite right. Many conditions, such as hypertension and diabetes, are so commonplace nowadays, that people often don't even consider themselves to have a 'disease' and will often forget to mention them when asked, so it can be helpful to ask, *"Any diabetes, high blood pressure, strokes….?"*

This happens a lot. Do not feel bad when this happens.

CHAPTER THREE:

Exams

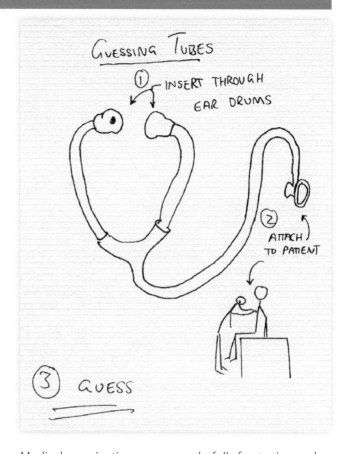

Medical examinations are a wonderfully frustrating and intimidating entity that become a routine part of life at medical school. You diligently learn what is essentially a poorly choreographed dance and perform it upon request in front of a consultant who hasn't done said dance since they themselves were at medical school. It's a rite of passage. You look blindly at the fingernails, praying the shaking is from your patient's hands and not your own, feel some pulses, and try to think of what you're going to do next while your stethoscope earbuds slowly pierce your tympani and your patient hyperventilates themselves into a pleasant delirium. The reality is that the diagnosis almost always comes from the history, and you're then supposed to examine to confirm what you think is going on. However, in order to know what 'examining' needs doing, you have to learn all the things there are to look, feel and listen for in the first place. Hence we have the dreaded OSCE routines to learn such as 'The Abdominal Examination'. At first the exams will seem unreasonably complicated and far too detailed to learn by heart, but I promise you that after years of practice with your med school friends, reminding yourself for the fiftieth time what the hell Janeway lesions are, you will eventually know them like the back of your warm, well-perfused, cap-refill-less-than-two-seconds, no splinter haemorrhages, koilonychia, onycholysis or leukonychia, no tar staining or clubbing… you get the point.

Abdominal exam

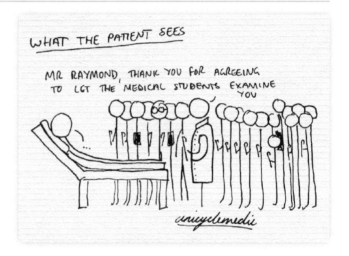

WHAT THE PATIENT SEES

MR RAYMOND, THANK YOU FOR AGREEING TO LET THE MEDICAL STUDENTS EXAMINE YOU

Mr Raymond's gloriously vast belly lay before me, distended and tense, an occasional cough sending ripples from his nipples to his pelvis. His sunken yellowed eyes had a broken kindness about them as he lay smiling at me in a warm and almost sympathetic manner; clearly I was not his first medical student.

"I'm not supposed to tell you I drink lots of beer" he chirped. *"Oh shit, whoops."*

I sniggered nervously as I squidged a glob of slimy cold hand gel into my sweating palms and wandered over to his bedside. I could feel the staring eyes of my fellow students who lined the wall of the cubicle, silently judging my frankly less-than-adequate performance. Introducing myself in that robotic way, *"Hello, my name is… I'm one of the medical students, would it be all right if…"*, I was interrupted gruffly by the consultant,

"Just feel his damned abdomen!"

I glanced at Mr Raymond, who nodded politely and popped his hands, which he had already held up for me to start with, back down by his side and let his head flop back onto the pillow. I laid my frighteningly cold hand on a random area of his domed midriff and began pushing gently. A strange firmness met my hand, as if resisting my attempts to palpate what lay beneath what was quite clearly a substantial amount of fluid that shouldn't really be there. Each time I squeezed my hand down, his belly would bulge elsewhere, like some perverse balloon animal, and no matter how hard I tried I couldn't feel any of the organs. I changed tack and decided to 'assess' for the fluid that was quite obviously present in abundance; tapping my palm on one side and feeling for a 'thrill' as the shock wave met my other hand on the other side. I say 'thrill' – you could have surfed that wave and it almost knocked my receiving hand clean off the bed.

"I believe this is a positive fluid thrill, and would suggest there is significant ascites," I calmly stated.

"Wonderful. Next!" retorted the consultant, as the next student shuffled in to throw Mr Raymond's abdomen around once more. One by one we were scanned through like groceries, giving a quick demonstration to show whether we had learned a single thing this rotation. I was just glad it was over. Half an hour later as I sat in the sun eating my sandwich, I pondered what I could have done to improve my examination technique. As I licked the last fleck of peanut butter off my finger I realised with a sigh I probably should have washed my hands.

Being able to perform a competent examination of the abdomen is one of the most important skills to accomplish at medical school. There are a lot of things that can go wrong within the abdomen, and equally there are many ways of determining what exactly is happening. Be systematic and thorough and don't jump to any conclusions. As with all examinations, the best way to become proficient is to practise until you find a routine that works for you. I'm strongly of the opinion that there is no one way to do an exam; rather it is a personal process that you develop over time with experience. Once you have found a way that you like to do it, do it the same way every time to reinforce it effectively. I'm not going to use this book to bore you with every single step as you'll have it presented to you in myriad different ways during your time at medical school. If you are interested in my method, I have written a comprehensive step-by-step guide which you can find by scanning the QR code in the margin; it's also available at bit.ly/SMabdo.

Pro tip: 💡

Always remember to look for hernias. They're really common.

What I will do is quickly mention the best advice I've received to help make it slick.

General inspection

This happened to me at med school, exactly as you see it. An esteemed consultant neurosurgeon asked me to perform a cerebellar examination on a young boy who had undergone resection of an occipital tumour, and once I'd finished, squared me up and calmly asked, "So how old is this patient?" which of course I hadn't anticipated being asked. I looked at the child, and took a guess. "Four".

"Look around."

Behind the child sat his rather embarrassed-looking parents, and draped all around the cubicle lay dozens of cards, balloons and gifts mockingly emblazoned with the number 5, some even with '5 today!' written on them.

Pro tip: 💡

Expose the abdomen, then step back and then do your inspection. Otherwise you won't see the huge scar and stoma bag that then explains why there's a bottle of Fortisip on the bedside table (malnutrition following bowel resection).

There's a lot to be gained from a really thorough initial inspection. Just having a look can tell you a lot about why a patient has come in. This is especially the case when it comes to OSCEs as they deliberately give you clues so they can assess whether you are inspecting at all. After a while you will be able to diagnose many conditions on inspection alone.

Colour is important in medicine, and there are four that I pay particular attention to for the abdominal examination:

▶ Blue – *cyanosis*

▶ Yellow – *jaundice*

▶ White – *anaemia*

▶ Grey – *excess iron, wizard, dead.*

In someone with dark skin it can be difficult to assess for anaemia. To get around this, look at their conjunctiva and oral mucosa, and ask them whether *they feel* that they look paler than normal.

Palpation

Pro tip: 💡

If the consultant can feel a spleen, it's already at least 50% enlarged. If a med student can feel a spleen it's probably at least 100% enlarged.

When palpating for the organs, use the middle section of your fingers so you're not digging into their skin, and use a gentle rocking motion like your hand is doing the worm across the abdomen.

If there's a distended abdomen, its 99.99% (maybe) likely that it's due to one of the following:

▶ Fluid

▶ Fat

▶ Faeces

▶ Foetus

▶ Flatus

▶ Fire (inflammatory mass)

▶ Further investigations needed soon (possible malignancy).

Percussion is a strange art form, widely said to have been devised by an Austrian winemaker in the 1700s to determine how much fluid was left in his barrel, but apparently some medical chap called Avicenna beat him to it and was actually using it in Asia for medical purposes a long time before that, so you can believe what you want really. If you're percussing something, push your non-tapping finger flat and firmly against the surface to be percussed, and then bounce the end of your tapping finger off the middle phalanx (finger bone). A lot of people don't push hard enough with the non-tapping hand and so don't hear anything, so don't be afraid to push a little harder if the patient is happy with it.

Pro tip: 💡

Before percussing the bladder, it's a good idea to ask your patient whether they need to urinate first. I won't tell you how I found that out but basically I now have nice new trainers.

Auscultation

Have a listen. Take the opportunity to feel like a real doctor, pop your tubes on, and sit quietly with the bell to their belly. Enjoy the brief moment of peace and quiet in a turbulent world of beeping and shouting as an opportunity to question your life choices, think about what's for lunch, and maybe quickly check to hear if their bowels are churning away.

▸ Bubbling and gurgling – *good*

▸ Silent or 'tinkly' – *bad; suggests obstruction or a paralysed bowel*

Sometimes you'll do an examination and discover a whole host of clinical findings that you can't seem to match together to form one diagnosis. Don't worry, this is fine, especially in an elderly population where most people have more than one problem going on at the same time. Calmly keep a mental note of what you find, and at the end when you're presenting, you can say, *"I'm not sure how these two / five / ten signs fit together exactly; however, I know the causes of clubbing are…, and the midline scar could suggest…"*

While you may not get completely full marks for a House-esque diagnosis, you'll demonstrate that you have methodically performed the examination and are thinking logically about what the signs you've elicited may suggest. Remember you're training to be a reliable, safe, dependable junior doctor, not a wizened consultant. That bit comes later.

Pro tip: 💡

Some people are just weird.

The cardiovascular exam

As with most things in medicine, nobody is born good at listening to the heart, it's just a case of practising as many times as you can until you become at least moderately proficient. Get your shiny guessing tubes out and listen to everyone who'll let you; friends, family, other medical students, the dog. To begin with you'll be able to confidently say…

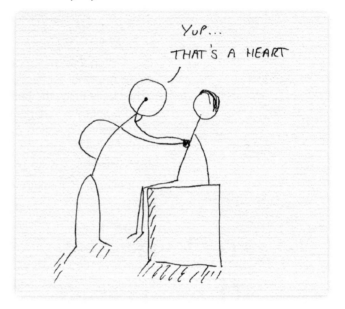

Enjoy the beauty of it. The heart has a mystical rhythm to it that is a delight to listen to as it diligently pounds away. Imagine the litres of blood passing through every minute, non-stop, for that person's entire life. Take time to appreciate the intricacies of the valves and conductive tissue ensuring the synchronicity of the contraction. It's magical. Gradually, with practice, you'll be able to detect the subtler sounds such as murmurs and clicks. Try feeling the pulse as you listen, to get a feel for which noises are systolic and which are diastolic. There's a lot of individual variation, so be sure to listen to lots of healthy people to get a feel for how broad 'normal' can be.

An important lesson

Sweating as usual, I closed my eyes in the vague hope that somehow it would improve my significantly sub-par auditory faculties as I desperately auscultated the rather large man's chest in Bed 2 on the cardiology ward round. The consultant had instructed each of us students to listen in turn, and as the last to go, it was now my turn. Amongst the somewhat inconvenient breath sounds the patient seemed to insist on making, I could hear the familiar rhythmic lub-dub, lub-dub, lub-dub of the man's ticker squelching away beneath his breastbone but that was it. I certainly couldn't convince myself I was able to hear a murmur of any kind. I shamefully drew my stethoscope away from his chest in defeat and shuffled back to my place in the line.

"Did you all hear the murmur?" boomed the consultant, expectantly, to which my suspiciously competent colleagues all bounced their heads in gleeful response. I didn't. I raised my hand a little, regretting my actions immediately as his razor-sharp gaze bore through my ignorant head. I felt six inches tall as he barked,

"Yes...?"

"Sorry, but I don't think I could hear the murmur." I was so unsure of myself that I was even unsure about *how* unsure I was. I prepared for the inevitable dressing down.

"Good."

I stood there, equally as baffled as my fellow students who were clearly let down at the missed opportunity to see one of their own torn limb from limb by an enraged senior.

"Pardon?"

"I said good. There isn't a murmur. And now I know which of my students are going to lie to me and say what they think I want to hear, rather than their actual clinical findings."

Well that was unexpected, I thought to myself somewhat smugly as I felt the barrel of the rifle slip away from me and onto my previously very chipper, now rather red, companions.

Never, ever, ever lie about what you think you can see, feel, hear or elicit in the form of clinical findings. Sure, it can be a bit concerning if a doctor can't hear a blaring ejection systolic murmur or a lung clogged to the brim with mucus, but as a student, nobody will ever be angry that you can't find something, in fact they'll actually be more inclined to help you try again if you're honest and say, *"nope, sorry"*. The worst thing to do is say that you can hear something when you can't, because not only do you miss out on the experience to learn how, but your seniors will not trust your judgement when it comes to actually examining and presenting if they know you are prone to making up clinical findings.

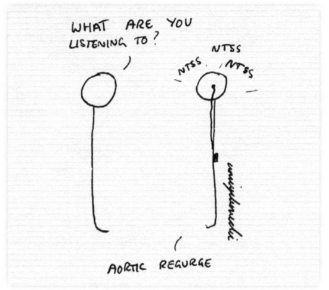

The respiratory exam

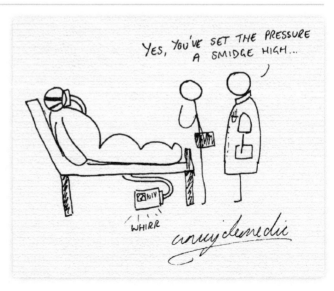

The respiratory exam is the longest of the major clinical examinations in medical school, and some would also argue that it's one of the most difficult as there is often a lot of information to gather and piece together in a short amount of time. It follows the same structure as all exams do of look, feel (percuss), and listen, and requires practice to make it slick enough to fit into the time frame during the OSCE. My top tips are as follows:

▸ Concentrate on the back, as most lung signs are found in the bases.

▸ Patients in exams generally have stable, long-term conditions, so swot up on your COPD, fibrosis, bronchiectasis and in (young people) cystic fibrosis facts.

▸ There are often more visual clues than other examinations, such as inhalers, oxygen cylinders, lobectomy scars and pursed lip breathing, so, as always, *take a good look around.*

> ### Pro tip:
>
> *Fremitus – if it's louder over a certain area of the lungs when they hum or say 'ninety-nine', then it means there's something more dense beneath the stethoscope than air, such as consolidation or a mass. If on the other hand it's really quiet, think of pneumothorax or pleural effusion.*

Orthopaedics

Orthopaedics is a subject that doesn't usually get all that much attention at medical school, especially given how huge a specialty it is. It's a field where most of the art is in the management, rather than the diagnosis, and its primary goal is retrieval of *function*.

Diagnosis in orthopaedics is usually imaging based, and most of the time, relatively simple – *if it moves and it shouldn't, and there's a crack on the X-ray, it's an orthopaedic problem.* The complexity arises when you say *"so what are you going to do to fix it?"*, at which point the orthopods all get very excited and start talking about Philos plates and tension band wiring. While a medical registrar will take particular delight in working out the complex diagnosis of a medical patient before initiating the agreed management, the orthopaedic registrar will enjoy mulling over what the management should be based on the agreed diagnosis.

Orthopaedic X-rays follow the rule of 2s.

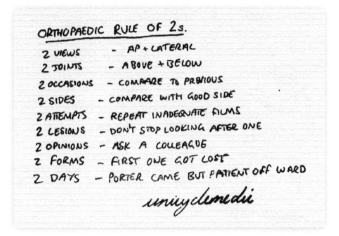

Pro tip:

You can yank really quite hard on joints without breaking the ligaments. You might, however, cause a lot of pain, so try to tailor it to your patient.

Pro tip: 💡

The most important orthopaedic emergency is compartment syndrome, where the pressures in the limb exceed blood pressure and compromise neurovascular supply to the limb. Wiggle their toes/fingers passively – if they scream, get help fast.

If anyone asks, modern joint replacements are not usually affected by MRI. You won't rip Mrs Jenkins' knee out nor will Mr White's shoulder fly across the ward. One thing to remember, however, is that a *very recently* replaced knee should avoid MRI, as the slight warming / microvibration effect can interrupt the healing process, so make sure you know how recent the implant is.

Rectal exam

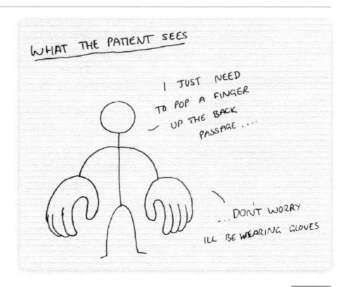

"You can probably take it out now," muttered the consultant dryly after watching me stand bewildered for rather a while with my index finger up the backside of an unfathomably patient patient. I had no idea what I was feeling for, whether I was doing it correctly, or when was socially appropriate to end this unique encounter with a complete stranger. I retracted my incarcerated digit and quickly wiped the glove on a piece of tissue before thanking the patient and hurrying off to wash my hands. Twice.

As a medical student it is a rite of passage to examine the… passage. To begin with you'll probably dread it, wondering why or how anyone could tolerate doing something like that regularly as part of their job. However, what you'll find is that as you get more experienced, and less perturbed by the insanity of the procedure, it becomes just another skill in your repertoire, and will cease to be something to fret about. After all, there are several very good reasons to do a digital rectal examination:

▶ Is there poo?

> The commonest cause of diarrhoea in an elderly patient is *overflow* diarrhoea. That means they're so incredibly constipated that the only thing that can make it past the solid, impacted stool in the rectum is liquid. Therefore if you can feel hard poo in the rectum, they need that clearing out somewhat urgently.

▶ Is there no poo?

> If someone has a distended painful abdomen, vomiting and constipation, you have to rule out intestinal obstruction. It could all be constipation, in which case you'd expect there to be poo in the rectum. If there is no poo, it suggests the blockage is higher up, and may even require surgery.

▶ Can they squeeze your finger?

> Cauda equina syndrome is an acute compression of the tail end of the spinal cord and can cause paralysis of the anal sphincter, indicating urgent need for neurosurgical intervention.

"No-one's done that to me in years…"

Pro tip: 💡

Patients sometimes make rather strange remarks after or even during rectal exams, often as an attempt to lighten the mood and shrug off any embarrassment. Just smile and wash your hands. Twice.

Pelvic exam

I have written a full script on how to do a successful pelvic exam on my blog at unicyclemedic.com if you're in the midst of trying to learn how to do it; you can scan the QR code in the margin to access this, or visit bit.ly/SMpelvic.

The pelvic exam is a scary one, because it's very intimate, and both you and the patient are nervous about what the other is going to think. I'll be completely honest from the off and say this, I am a *very* junior doctor and have done this *very* few times, so I am most certainly not an expert. However, I did learn two critical things from those few times that I have performed this exam.

Thing #1

Make sure the woman feels in control. She is in a vulnerable position, and is trusting you to maintain her dignity, not to hurt her, and to show that her trust in you is not misplaced. You also don't know what experiences she has had in the past that may make it psychologically difficult to allow someone to examine her. As a result she is likely to be very nervous. To begin with, as with any exam or procedure that has the potential to be 'awkward', make sure you have a chaperone, preferably female in this case. The next thing is to say:

"Remember that you're in charge – you don't have to do anything you don't want to. If you say 'Stop' at any point, I will stop immediately."

Knowing they're in control can make all the difference in the world.

Pro tip:

A surprise sneeze can send a speculum across the room. Embarrassing stuff does happen, and that's okay, just make sure the patient knows you aren't bothered in the slightest by it.

Thing #2

Open the speculum very, very slowly. The vaginal walls are able to stretch easily enough to accommodate the speculum without causing pain. If you open it too quickly it will cause the pelvic floor muscles to spasm and the patient won't like you very much. Take your time.

Fundoscopy

I have only ever been able to deduce two things from looking in the back of a patient's eyes:

1. This patient has eyes

2. I'm not very good at fundoscopy.

Fundoscopy is *hard*. I don't like getting that close to a stranger's face and I always get unreasonably stressed out and sweaty when I can't see anything in the back of the eye. I have never seen papilloedema and I've never seen retinal detachment, but I have seen blood vessels and red reflexes, so I guess that's something. What does this mean for me in the clinical environment? It means exactly two things:

1. If a patient has an eye problem, I am *always* going to ask a senior for a second opinion

2. If a patient has an eye problem, I am *always* going to have a go at looking in the eye myself.

Being not very good at something isn't a reason not to do it. It's precisely the reason to do it as much as possible. As I mentioned earlier on, one of the things I love about medicine is that nobody is 'innately' good at it, like drawing or singing; instead you just have to do it again and again until you're reasonably experienced. So look in the back of the eye whenever you get the chance. Even if you don't see anything, the patient will feel better for having had a seriously thorough examination.

Pro tip: 💡

Hold the ophthalmoscope in your good hand and put your other hand on their forehead (warn them first). This will let you feel how close you are to their face without bashing into their potentially already painful eye.

Snellen charts are great for assessing visual acuity. Make sure they cover one eye, and read the lowest line that they can see. Then get them to read from right to left for the other eye. This stops them remembering and repeating what they said before when actually they *can't* make out the same line with the bad eye.

Always good to ask.

Presenting – it's terrifying

I stood there, shaking a little as usual, while the grey-haired and equally grey-mannered consultant, in his characteristic braces and bow tie, looked at me with that curious blend of boredom and disdain that only comes with having been in the same position oneself, many years ago. I started to present my case,

"This patient has chest pain but I'm not convinced whether it's cardiac in origin and I've looked at the ECG and she's in atrial fibrillation but she says that's new…"

"Stop!"

I stopped. The familiar bead of sweat began its merry way down my spine and my knees seemed to suddenly require conscious effort to remain standing. Clearly I needed some more practice. The consultant's steely eyes gripped mine as he calmly began,

"Mrs Jones is an 82-year-old with an extensive cardiac history presenting with chest pain…"

His eloquence was unfathomable as he gently laid out all the information on a platter for me, a diagnostic buffet of clues and hints, and by the time he had finished, I knew this woman was most likely having a heart attack but we also needed to rule out a pulmonary embolism. It was just like answering an exam question that I had seen many times in the past. He smiled dryly and simply quipped, *"Good"*.

Presenting to a colleague, and particularly a senior, can feel like a panicked rush to blurt out as much information as quickly as possible, but in reality you are trying to guide their thought process as smoothly as possible, by laying out the information logically and methodically. There are limitless possibilities as to what could be wrong with someone walking through the door, so instead of trying to jump straight to what you think the answer is, you whittle your way down by gradually building a picture of the patient, cutting out things that it *can't* be, until you're only left with a couple of options.

1. Name, age, occupation

This is the usual way to start, as immediately you narrow down the possible diagnoses hugely. An 82-year-old woman with significant asbestos exposure from her job in construction is going to have vastly different health problems to a boy born three days ago.

2. Presenting complaint

What's the *main* reason they've come in? Much of the time patients will mention multiple symptoms, so asking *"what's the most worrying symptom, the pain or the breathlessness?"* is often a good tactic to employ.

3. Background

This is hugely important, because it tells you the patient's risk factors, and thus what they're most likely to get. Sudden onset chest pain in a 50-year-old obese smoker with a history of two heart attacks and peripheral vascular disease is almost certainly another heart attack, but the same symptom in a 20-year-old seven-foot rugby player is more likely a pneumothorax.

4. History of presenting complaint

What happened leading up to this person seeking medical attention? This is when you start to fill in the details and pad it out a bit to give a clearer picture of what might be going on. Is the pain gripping or stabbing? Does it radiate anywhere? Any associated symptoms such as clamminess, dizziness or vomiting?

5. Rest of the history

Social history, family history, other things – for completeness really. To be honest your consultant will have stopped listening after point number three, but it's good to be thorough.

Pro tip: 💡

For OSCEs you're presenting a history with the aim of answering the question "what's the diagnosis?" whereas in the clinical environment you're aiming more for "what do I need to rule out, and what investigations do I need to do?"

SBAR REFERRAL

S: SUMMON COURAGE TO PICK UP PHONE

B: BLURT OUT ALL THE MEDICAL WORDS YOU KNOW

A: AGREE TO ALL THE INSULTS THROWN AT YOU

R: REPLACE HANDSET. CRY.

SBAR is an effective way to hand over concise information to another professional, and you will get better with practice, I promise. Situation, Background, Assessment, Recommendation. Essentially, what is going on, what led up to it, what you think is happening and what you reckon is the best plan of action.

Making a diagnosis

IF YOU HEAR HOOVES, YOU DON'T ASSUME ZEBRAS

You will hear this many times throughout your medical career:

Common things are common.

If you hear hoofbeats, it's probably horses, and not zebras or in this case reindeer. If the patient is short of breath, coughing up gunk and has high temperatures, it's probably pneumonia, and probably *not* atypical pulmonary alveolar proteinosis.

As a medical student, you are training to become a doctor. You will start to see patients, take histories, examine and begin making diagnoses. You will start to have *your own patients*. It is a terrifying honour that isn't to be taken lightly. Once you have summoned up the courage to ask some questions of your patient, feel their belly and listen to what you hope is their lungs, you'll be asked what you think is going on with your patient. What do *you* feel is the diagnosis, based on the years of study that you have dedicated to your craft? Pneumonia? Bowel obstruction? The flu?

Often you won't know. That's absolutely fine. What you must do is commit to something. Even if you're not sure, decide what you think is *most likely*, and put your name to it. Imagine you are the only doctor in the hospital available to treat this person, and *make your diagnosis, Doctor!*

Why? Because that's what you have to do as a junior doctor. You will, at some point, have to start making decisions without a senior immediately available to guide you, and you will often be right. You will also often get it wrong, and as a medical student you will then be told why you're wrong, and the real diagnosis will be revealed to you, and that's how you learn effectively.

The emotional investment of putting yourself out there and committing to a diagnosis, realising that this means you could well be wrong, and potentially being called out on it, ensures you will remember it much better than if you were to ask someone for the correct answer before making a decision. That feeling of fear as you suggest your idea to the stern-looking consultant in front of you is the same adrenaline that is going to burn that correct diagnosis into your memory forever.

Embrace the fear!

Describing a lesion

Very often as a junior doctor you'll be the first one who has seen a rash, lump or lesion, and the consultant will ask you about it before seeing it in person. It's very tempting to think *"Ah well, the consultant will come and see it in a minute"* and not really examine a lesion properly, but one day you're going to be the one in charge and that decision-making experience only comes with experience.

If you get into the habit of noting a few specific things about each and every lesion you see, you'll usually have enough information to make the diagnosis, or at least enough for the consultant to value your input.

I use the ridiculous acronym of **SSLOI CMPOTA:**

(phonetically it's *Sloy-compoter*)

- Size – in centimetres
- Shape – circular, oval, irregular
- Location – inner aspect of upper arm, posterior aspect of scalp
- Outline – smooth, craggy, well-demarcated, difficult to establish
- Illumination – glows if you stick a pen torch against it (fluid-filled)
- Consistency – hard, firm, fluctuant, boggy
- Mobility – mobile, fixed, adherent to underlying skin

▸ Pulsatility – can you feel a pulse, or a buzzing? (vascular lesion)

▸ Overlying skin – red and inflamed, tethered to lump

▸ Temperature – hot, body temperature, ischaemically cold

▸ Auscultation – bruits, pulse, bowel sounds

There are very few lumps and bumps that can't be diagnosed using the above information, and you'll seriously impress a senior if you calmly and confidently crack out,

"There is a 3cm irregular lump on the upper outer aspect of the breast that doesn't illuminate and is craggy and hard. It is fixed to the underlying tissue, non-pulsatile and with no obvious overlying skin reaction. It's not hot and I can't hear any bruits."

Doesn't matter in the slightest if you don't know the diagnosis. The consultant now does, and they also know that you know your stuff.

For determining size, a useful thing to do is to measure your hands. Get a tape measure and work out the width of your fingertips, the distance between tip of thumb and index finger, and between thumb and little finger with your hand spread as far as it can. *Voilà*, you have three useful tools for measuring lumps and rashes. If you can confidently say it's a 3cm lump rather than 'about 5cm' it sounds much more impressive.

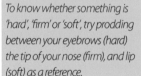

Pro tip:

To know whether something is 'hard', 'firm' or 'soft', try prodding between your eyebrows (hard) the tip of your nose (firm), and lip (soft) as a reference.

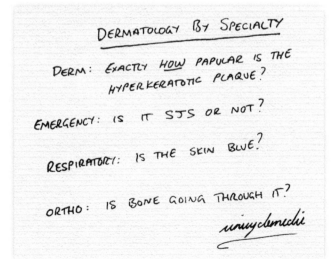

DERMATOLOGY BY SPECIALTY

DERM: EXACTLY HOW PAPULAR IS THE HYPERKERATOTIC PLAQUE?

EMERGENCY: IS IT SJS OR NOT?

RESPIRATORY: IS THE SKIN BLUE?

ORTHO: IS BONE GOING THROUGH IT?

There will be many times when you forget to ask a question and have to go back. This is fine, and most patients actually appreciate the extra time with you. In exams, however, it's a little different, and you won't get a second chance to ask the patient questions, so it's good to get a well-rehearsed structure to your history-taking to avoid missing important information.

CHAPTER FOUR:

Procedures

New procedures are scary, and will feel firmly outside of your comfort zone. This will continue throughout your medical career and you will gradually get used to pushing your boundaries. It's a rare thing to find a career that forces you to learn so much so quickly. The important thing is to make sure you're safe.

If you're not happy doing something, ask for help. There are no prizes for pride.

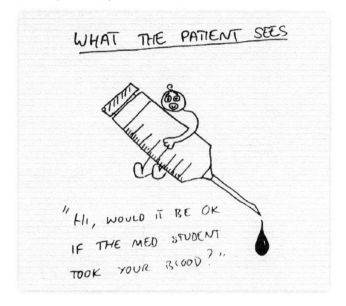

Pro tip:

For lumbar punctures, always measure the opening pressure. This may be the only parameter that suggests encephalitis that would otherwise go unnoticed. But remember the patient must be lying down! Otherwise the upright spinal column with the reservoir of fluid at the top in the brain will ensure their pressure will be artificially high – often ridiculously so.

Aspirate the needle

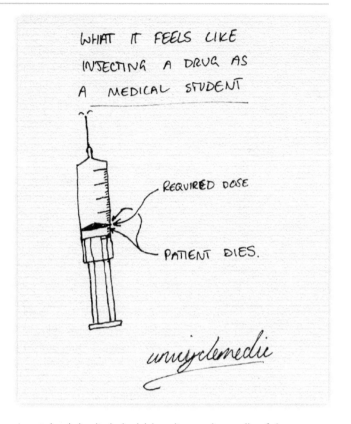

I watched the little bubbles slip up the walls of the syringe as I drew up the lidocaine, my shaking hand announcing to the world that this was clearly my first time administering local anaesthetic. Fortunately, the wound was on the patient's scalp and he was facing the other way, so it was just me and the registrar witnessing my incompetence, but I was fairly sure this wasn't new information to him anyway. I swapped the drawing up needle for the sharp green one and turned to the patient. As I slid the needle into the skin, the registrar calmly said, *"pause"*.

I paused.

"Aspirate a little." I did. To my surprise a beautiful wisp of red darted into the syringe as the plunger drew back, blood staining the clear anaesthetic I had spent several minutes wrestling into the tube. *"That's not supposed to happen,"* I mumbled to myself. I was shaking a lot now.

"That's why you aspirate – to see if you're in a vessel. Pull the needle out and try somewhere else". I shamefacedly withdrew the needle, and slid it once again into the poor man's scalp. I say poor – he was clearly enjoying the sizeable dose of ketamine that had been administered earlier and didn't seem all that fussed by the ordeal. This time the plunger wouldn't budge, and the registrar gave me the nod to inject the anaesthetic into the skin. The skin blebbed up nicely and I got my sign-off. Happy days.

Whenever doing anything involving a syringe and a patient, be sure to do one thing if nothing else. Aspirate the needle a little before pushing the plunger. Literally no bad things can happen if you pull back on that plunger. Either it will resist and nothing will happen (in which case you're not in a fluid-filled vessel or cavity), or it will start to fill up with something (blood, air, urine…), in which case you most certainly are within a cavity or vessel. This allows you to reposition the needle and try again.

On the other hand, literally terrible things can happen if you start shoving fluids or drugs through a needle whose exact location you're unsure about, especially when giving local anaesthetic. Make a habit of aspirating first, and your patient won't fall apart because you've just filled their heart with the lidocaine that was supposed to stay in the skin.

Pro tip: 💡

If you're trying to get the tip of the needle into a vein, and the patient has very loose skin and wriggly veins, try using your non-dominant hand to hold their arm and with the thumb, gently drag the skin until it's as taut as you can get it. Sometimes that's enough to hold the vein in place long enough to get that blasted needle in.

ABG

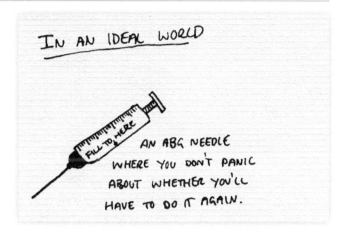

In an ideal world

AN ABG NEEDLE
WHERE YOU DON'T PANIC
ABOUT WHETHER YOU'LL
HAVE TO DO IT AGAIN.

FILL TO HERE

Okay, ABGs are scary. The first time I attempted the frankly maniacal challenge of putting a needle into someone's *artery* I was a third-year medical student on my cardio-respiratory rotation and before me sat a wheezing, gasping behemoth of a man called Alan. He was a veteran truck driver who'd become suddenly short of breath at the wheel and had been admitted with acute heart failure. My job now was to retrieve blood from his radial artery to decide whether or not our treatment was improving his blood oxygen saturations. The final-year student assisting me demonstrated to me the technique, handed me the needle and calmly announced,

"Crack on."

I felt for the pulse, slid the needle in, and waited. A beautiful column of bright red blood slid up the barrel of the syringe and it took all my self-control not to shout with joy.

"That bloody hurt, you bastard," Alan reprimanded me between gasps. I breathed a sigh of relief, withdrew the needle and pressed hard over the puncture site for a good two minutes while my colleague went and ran the sample to the machine. I felt awesome. It was my first ever attempt at doing an arterial sample and I had *nailed* it. I was the best, a natural talent clearly. I promptly and confidently failed the next four that I tried but that's beside the point.

In terms of technique, when doing an ABG, I find it easiest to rest my right wrist in the patient's hand, and cock their wrist right back so the palmar side is stretched nice and taught. I use my right index finger, pointed up towards their elbow, to feel for the radial pulse while the rest of my fingers hold their hand still. I choose a point where I can feel the pulse that is as close to the wrist as possible, as this is where the radial artery is most superficial. Then I take the needle in my right hand, held like a pen with bevel side up and with the plunger retracted to allow blood to fill the barrel, and slide it in gently at 45 degrees-ish. If no blood comes out, I wait, take a couple of breaths, retract the needle until it's just under the skin, and try a slightly different angle of approach. If in doubt, the artery is usually a little medial to where you think it is.

We've all failed many, many ABGs and we've all felt absolutely terrible about it. It's incredibly frustrating when you know you're causing the patient pain and all you want is to find that damned blood vessel that you swear you were right on top of a second ago. It's okay, patients will forgive you, and as you'll read later, you get used to failing, it's part of the job.

Pro tip: 💡

Not all ABG syringes will 'self-fill', so pull back the plunger before inserting the needle.

ECGs

The entire nurses' station dissolved into panic on a relatively mundane Tuesday afternoon as Bed 4's cardiac monitor trace suddenly flatlined. We hit the alarm, grabbed the crash trolley and ran round to his cubicle to find that he'd unplugged the leads and gone for a smoke.

Common things are common.

ECGs are scary strips of this strange new language that you must learn to read and interpret, and depending on how fluent you are, may mean the difference between life and death in a patient with chest pain. As a medical student I used to watch in awe as the seasoned registrar would glance for three seconds at the flimsy pink paper handed to him by the nurse and say, *"Yeah that's fine"* before dealing with task number 53 of the morning.

The trick is not to rush, especially early on, and to be methodical and thorough, inspecting each section as a matter of routine – rate, rhythm, axis, P wave, PR interval, QRS complex, QT interval, ST segment, T waves. Gradually you'll become more proficient at reading them, but make sure you do it the same way each time so as not to miss stuff. Nobody will be angry at you if you're slow but careful.

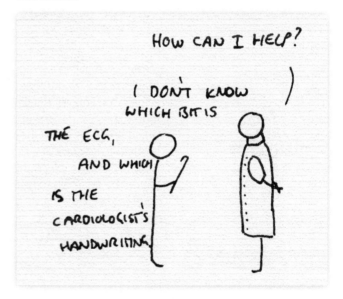

It also doesn't help when they've scrawled words you've never seen before like *'Concealed extrasystolic ventricular bigeminy with interpolation'*.

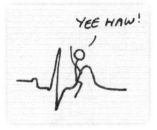

Many ECG machines generate an 'auto-report' at the top of the page, saying things like *'sinus rhythm with frequent ectopics'* or *'abnormal ECG'*. In general you're taught to ignore these and make up your own mind about what's going on. To be fair to the machine, it does have a pretty decent crack at it but it doesn't know the clinical circumstances in which the ECG has been taken so cannot be assumed to give a reliable diagnosis.

Don't forget the PR interval.

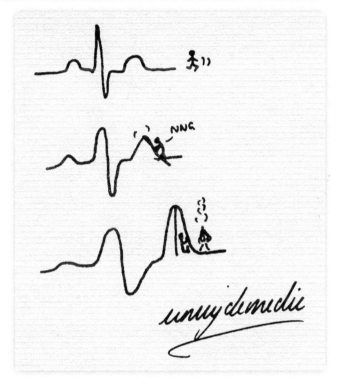

How I remember the ECG features of hyperkalaemia: flattened P waves, broad QRS, tall 'tented' T waves.

Imaging

Chest X-rays

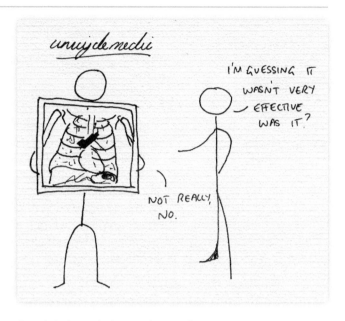

Poor inhaler technique is the number one reason patients complain that their inhaler 'doesn't work'.

Chest X-rays are the most commonly requested imaging modality, and for good reason. They are very useful, very easy, very cheap and require only a minimal dose of radiation to pass through what is essentially an air-filled chest cavity. See as many as you can, and you'll gradually get to grips with how variable 'normal' can be. As with all tests and investigations, the key is to develop a routine and be thorough. Most people remember to look at the lung fields, but many forget to check for an edge that suggests a pneumothorax, or to look through the heart to see if a cannonball renal cell metastasis is hiding there. A good way to do it is to think of all the structures that you know of in the thorax and have a look for them to see if they're abnormal, and don't forget to scan the bones quickly. It's worryingly frequent that a particularly stoical patient's broken humeral head is only noticed because their chest X-ray revealed the fracture.

Pro tip:

Old, frail people with multiple diseases can have pretty gnarly looking chest X-rays. The trick is to bring up one from a few months or even years ago. If nothing has changed, then there's probably not much new to worry about.

Abdominal X-rays

"Tell me what you think of this abdominal X-ray."

"I can see that… I need to revise abdominal X-rays."

Chest radiographs are phenomenal in terms of how much information they can provide, given how simple and easy they are to perform. Abdominal films are also useful, but less commonly used as there are fewer indications for ordering them, and they don't give the same wealth of information that a chest film can. They're also a much heftier dose of radiation than to the chest, as instead of shooting through the largely air-filled lungs, there's a whole lot (often a huge amount) of soft tissue to penetrate. Nevertheless, it's essential that you can look at one without panicking, and get a rough idea about what's going on inside that patient of yours.

Indications – *'Gases, masses, bones and stones'*:

▶ Obstructed bowel

▶ Perforated bowel

▶ Bowel ischaemia

▶ Blunt or perforating abdominal injury

▶ Intussusception

▶ Foreign bodies

▶ Suspected abdominal mass

▶ Acute and chronic pancreatitis

▶ Toxic megacolon.

Step 1: The basics

Start with the obvious things. Have you got the right patient, at the right time (most recent scan) with the right view (adequate penetration and coverage)?

Step 2: Gases 3, 6, 9

Small bowel shouldn't be more than 3cm in diameter (any more suggests severe distension) and has complete rings called *valvulae conniventes* that cross the width of the tube. Large bowel has *haustra* that only go part way across. Large bowel shouldn't exceed 6cm, or 9cm at the caecum.

The reason we worry about the distension is highlighted by Laplace's law. The greater the radius of a tube, the more stress there is on the wall at a given pressure. This means a distended bowel is much, much more likely to rupture, and potentially cause life-threatening peritonitis.

Rigler's sign, where you can see dark lines along both sides of a wall of intestine, is a sign of intraperitoneal gas, and may reflect perforation or penetrating trauma that has allowed air into the peritoneal cavity. This may also be shown by air under the diaphragm, but that's usually seen on the chest X-ray.

Step 3: Masses

Solid organs such as liver, spleen and kidneys are technically visible on abdominal X-rays but often hard to see. Have a look where you think they are, and you might spot a particularly enlarged organ or growth.

Step 4: Bones

Briefly check the ribs, spine, sacrum and pelvis for fractures, wear and tear and cysts.

Pro tip: 💡

If you're looking at a strange foreign body and wondering what this person managed to swallow, consider whether it might be a piercing.

Step 5: Stones

Stones can pop up in lots of places, but you should check the kidneys and the ureters particularly. To find these, simply follow the tips of the lumbar transverse processes down to the sacroiliac joint, and the ischial spines mark where the ureters enter the bladder.

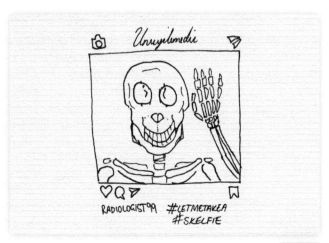

NG tube

When I look back at the first time I tried to insert a nasogastric tube into a patient, I simultaneously want to laugh and cry with remorse. It was the most catastrophically ridiculous event that will forever remain scarred across my cortex to remind me just how strange a job medicine can prove to be.

Pro tip:

If you're putting an NG tube in to feed someone, you must get an X-ray to confirm the tip is in the stomach and not curled up in a lung before you start putting food down it and give them a cracking pneumonitis.

Mr White was sat quietly on HDU recovering from some sort of abdominal surgery, and the recent rearrangement of his internal organs had left him with post-operative ileus, meaning his bowel had gone to sleep. As an inevitable consequence his stomach had decided to send all gastric contents northwards with spectacular vigour. The NG tube was supposed to decompress the stomach and help relieve the vomiting by draining the gunk. The premise is very simple – you measure the tube length from their lips, around the ear and down to the xiphisternum. Then you give them a glass of water and tell them to take a sip and hold it in their mouth. You then slide the tube through the nose to the back of their throat, they swallow the water and you shove the tube, riding the wave of the swallow, all the way down to the stomach. Easy.

Or not. What actually happened on my first attempt was remarkably different to the instruction manual. To begin with the man's right nostril was so blocked with snot and crust that it wouldn't let the tube past. The left was marginally better but by the time I'd slid the slippery worm of a tube down to his nasopharynx, he'd drunk all the water. Apparently I hadn't explained it right, so I speedily nipped out to get another glass, but when I returned, the tube was on the floor and Mr White was asleep. I sighed. Second tube, in the nostril, glass of water, ready to go… vomit. Lots of it, mainly on my shoes. Removing the tube, I called for some help from the terribly sympathetic nurse who had clearly seen many a medical student struggle before, and she calmly and quietly showed me how it was done. Maybe next time I'd do it all by myself…

Point the tube straight back along the base of the nostril, not up into the head. When the patient can feel it (ask them) at the back of their throat, get them to take one big swallow of water, and give a really good shove as they do so. Confidence is key. Once you're past the gag reflex you can gently slide it the rest of the way. If they're gagging, you're in the oesophagus. If they're coughing, you may be in the trachea and should pull back and try again.

Pro tip:

Refrigerate the tube beforehand, to stiffen it a little.

CHAPTER FIVE:

Life on the wards

Surviving the ward round

The dreaded ward round commenced at 08.00. You were buzzing, coffee swilling warmly through your veins, notebook and pen at the ready; a diligent student of a glorious vocation, ready to learn. It's now 09.45 and you're stealing guilty glances at the clock, your weary eyes sliding down to your crumpled patient list to see how much more of this ordeal remains to be endured. A mortifyingly audible rumble emanates from your midriff as the consultant falls silent to auscultate yet another wheezing chest. A whiff of barrier cream tickles your nostrils and you feel that all-too-familiar wave of disappointment wash over you as you realise the round is less than a third of the way through, complemented by a trickle of frustration at the dogged determination of the patient who just won't stop asking questions. You watch in awe the junior doctors relentlessly scribbling away in the notes, rifling through drug charts like finely-honed machines, the registrar occasionally handing you snippets of useful information and asking ego-destroying questions like *"Can you name the 24 causes of clubbing…?"*

How do they survive these things? How are they not *starving*? Are they even human?

Ward rounds suck. Nobody likes them, not even the consultant, and they're in charge of the damn things. You're tired, hungry, bored, you don't understand what's going on and you're scared you'll be asked difficult questions. And that's what the F1 is feeling, let alone the med student.

You will be told time and again by wizened bespectacled seniors that being present on the ward round, following the medical team as they trudge from complex patient to complex patient, is a valuable and vital part of your learning as a student. Well it's not. It's a soul-destroying waste of time that only serves to remind you how little you know and how boring ward rounds are.

What actually *is* useful is actively trying to get just one positive thing from each round, that will stick with you forever. Just one. For example – for every patient you see on the round on one day, have a look at their catheter if they have one. Just admire the yellow (or not) fluid, see if there's anything in there (pus, grit, blood…); how much have they passed? Do they look dehydrated? That's it. Just one thing on that day, and do it for all the patients you see. You'll notice some are passing lots of clear urine, others less and much more concentrated. Some won't have catheters at all, which means that hopefully they don't need one, and are able to pass urine. But how much? Does the consultant or any other member of the team ask the patient how much they're passing? It's something that often gets missed, yet can be an incredibly useful way of monitoring someone's kidney function as well as their overall health and recovery.

Different day, different focus – are they eating and drinking? What can they manage? What you'll find is that as well as the new topic you've chosen, you'll naturally also quickly check their catheter, because you got into the habit of doing it the day before. This way, by gradually building up one by one, you'll soon find yourself doing an entire check through all of the patient's parameters without even thinking about it, and the ward round becomes a lot more interesting!

Things to check:

▸ Catheters and fluid balance

▸ Bowels and food intake

▸ Wounds and dressings

▸ Oxygen requirements

▸ Pain control

▸ Blood results, such as haemoglobin and inflammatory markers

▸ Mobility and how they're getting on with the physiotherapy team

▸ Mood

▸ Regular medications

▸ TED stockings and dalteparin prescription

Grilling

Also known as 'pimping', grilling has earned itself legendary status among medical students as an experience to be feared and avoided. The ward round falls quiet as the predatory eyes of the consultant slide to meet yours. Locked in. Target acquired.

"And what would you want to investigate in a patient with S. bovis *endocarditis?"*

Clunk.

"… their heart?"

Solid suggestion there, champ. Three years of medical school and the only answer you can give to 'what should you look at in someone with a heart problem?' is 'their heart' – frankly pitiful. As all of the moisture that was previously on my tongue somehow disappears and reappears in my palms, the consultant's eyebrows return to their usual position, ready for the dressing down.

> **Pro tip:** 💡
>
> *The answer is* **colonoscopy***, as* S. bovis *endocarditis often results from bacterial translocation following damage to the bowel wall caused by malignancy. Neat, eh?*

Weirdly I'm someone who likes being put on the spot in front of the ward round and grilled for a response to questions I could never have hoped to answer, while the entirety of the medical team watch me quietly drown in my own ignorance. *"…Er …why?…"* you ask – because in that moment, when the adrenaline is scouring the lining off the inside of your arteries and your shirt becomes eerily moist, your brain goes into survival mode, slowing down time, increasing alertness and remembering **everything** as if your life depended on it. I have found it to be without question the most efficient way to learn new information. Get grilled on a topic once, and not know the answer, and you'll never forget it again. Just remember to breathe afterwards.

THE REVERSAL MOMENT

THE POINT IN TIME WHEN THE MEDICAL STUDENT ON THE WARD ROUND BEGINS CONTEMPLATING WHETHER THEY WOULD CONSIDER SWAPPING PLACES WITH THE PATIENT IN FRONT OF THEM.

The rule of mum

Very simple, and my most important rule. Whenever you are about to interact with a patient or other member of staff, or even to go out in public, ask yourself the following:

"What would I want the doctor looking after my mother to do in this situation?"

By thinking for just a brief moment about the qualities you'd like to see in the doctor looking after your nearest and dearest, you may well find yourself making more responsible and professional choices. Maybe you'll take a minute longer to make sure your patient understands what you've said, or tuck in Mrs Jones' feet so they don't get cold, or even just slide Mr Gibbs' table close enough so he can reach his water that the previous doctor moved away when they listened to his chest. You'll be amazed at the profound impact that one question can have on your own behaviour, so give it a go, and I promise it'll make you feel better. Which brings me nicely onto…

Remember the little things

My consultant during my surgical rotation in final year was a glorious man. Tall, graceful and impeccably clean-shaven, he reigned supreme when it came to Hartmann's procedures, resecting with perfect margins and in record time the vile malignancy that was crippling Ms Richard's insides, thereby saving her from impending death and granting her a new lease of life. Hero. So imagine his surprise when we whisked back the curtain and she smiled at *me* and thanked me for everything that *I'd* done!

What I had in fact done was adjust her pillows and bring her a fresh cup of tea after her operation, because the nurses were so busy she hadn't anyone to help her. As a medical student I often felt I couldn't contribute much to the medical team. Everyone else knew a lot more than me, and was more competent with procedures, and so I spent much of my time following them around all day like a lost duckling.

What I realised was there was something I had a lot more of than them, which I could use to my advantage – *time*. I had so much more time than the junior doctors to talk to patients, to ask them how they were feeling or if I could do anything for them, and what I discovered was game-changing. Patients were just as grateful to me for sitting and chatting for a few minutes, passing them their phone charger that they'd been trying to reach for an hour, or getting a fresh cup of tea, as they were for the medical care they were receiving from the team. I got to know my patients much better; I could start suggesting things on the round like, *"Mr Jones has been feeling really nauseous with the morphine but he hasn't wanted to mention it"* which would then prompt a change in their management.

I was contributing!

The absolute highlight was with a patient called Ken who everyone had labelled as an angry and generally nasty individual who wouldn't engage with the medical team or listen to the doctors, and thus little time was spent on the ward round with him. I sat and listened to him for a while – he told me about his family and his previous job as a magician, and how he was scared to ask questions about his care because he felt he'd be ridiculed or dismissed for not 'keeping up'. I asked him what his concerns were and mentioned them to the consultant the next morning on the round. As we entered his bay he waved at me cheerily, saying,

"Hello mate!"

The entire team stopped and looked at me as if I'd just spoken Parseltongue.

"Did Ken just call you 'mate'?" muttered the registrar.

"Apparently so."

For the first time ever as a medical student I felt like a truly valuable member of the team, whose communication with a patient had improved their relationship with the team, their outlook on their illness, and ultimately the quality of the care they received. And all I'd done was sit and listen for a bit.

Pro tip:

When listening to an angry patient, if they are complaining about the hospital or the doctors, don't try to defend or explain, just listen. Keep listening until they have nothing else to say. Usually they'll fizzle out, realise we're all doing our best to help, and will often thank you for your time. A large part of why patients feel disgruntled is because they don't feel listened to. As a medical student you are uniquely able to fill that role.

The man in Bed 3

> PATIENT NAME: MARK JONES
>
> BED No.: C3
>
> NURSE: ANNIE / CLAIRE
>
> LIKES TO BE CALLED : CHAP WITH THE ABSCESS

"What happened to Mr Jones?" I asked of a particularly caffeinated registrar during the third week of my rotation on surgery.

"Who?"

"The man in Bed three."

"Nope"

"Chap with the abscess?"

"Ah yes, he went to theatre for washout and debridement and is recovering well in HDU."

This happens a lot. The sheer number of patients that are processed through the healthcare system every day means it can be hard to remember abstract things like names, as they have no real relevance to the patient's management, kind of like shoe size or what car they drive. Their pathology is what is of relevance, interest and importance, and is what their doctor is thinking about most, so don't be surprised when patients become known by their pathology in meetings and on ward rounds.

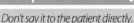

Pro tip:

Don't say it to the patient directly.

Therapy dog

Therapy dog day is the best day.

I sat on my creaky kindergarten chair on the elderly care ward and watched with a ridiculous grin on my face as the chocolate labrador puppy flopped its joyful way around the musty room. One by one the creaking, rasping patients leant forward to run their hands along its glistening fur, their smiles as big as mine. The look on their faces said it all. Medicine isn't just about piling pills and drugs into our patients, we have to treat them as a whole – body and soul. That little ball of fur was making them happier than any of their medications ever could, and for many of the people in the room (myself included) it was the highlight of their week.

Pro tip:

Treat your patient, not the disease!

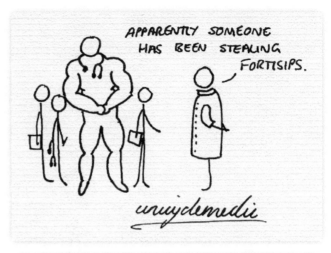

Remember that the goal of medicine is to promote health as well as fix disease – prevention is always the best management if possible.

CPR

TURNS OUT YOU GET BETTER RESULTS BY INJECTING THE ADRENALINE INTO THE MED STUDENT

unwjclimedic

The first time I performed CPR on a real live (dead) human being was in my fourth year of medical school on my emergency placement. I'd practised on the models as we'd been instructed, and felt that I understood fairly well what to expect when doing it for real.

I didn't.

There is no simulation that will adequately prepare you for the sensation of breaking someone's ribs as you try to pummel life back into their grey, motionless body. It is a brutal, disturbing and undignified affair that very rarely works, and always takes an emotional toll that sits with you for a long while after. But when it does work, and you see that taunting cardiac monitor quiver back into a perfusing rhythm, and the chest gasp back into motion, that feeling of relief is second to none.

Get involved. Make sure you've done CPR on a real dead person at least once before you qualify as a doctor. Feel just how hard you have to force the chest down into the bed to achieve adequate compression to supply the brain with barely-oxygenated blood. Feel the fear as brittle osteoporotic ribs crack beneath your sweating hands and the adrenaline courses through your pounding arteries as you realise you haven't taken a breath in almost a minute. Learn to hold your arms straight, hinge at the hips, and how to change over effectively with a colleague when you get tired. Witness the futility, how everyone in the room watches the monitor with that fading glimmer of hope that the trace may flicker back to life, while simultaneously hoping the clinician running the resuscitation calls it sooner rather than later to save the patient from suffering any longer. Watch the consultant take the family aside to tell them that we did everything we could, see them cry, see the nurses clearing up afterwards as everyone attempts to return to their normal working day. You have to see it to understand. You have to feel the hole in your insides as you realise that you just watched a life end. Make sure that happens while you're a student. It makes it just that bit easier when you're responsible for that person as a doctor.

Pro tip: 💡

There's no place for pride in CPR. Swap with a colleague after a maximum of two cycles.

Document or die

If it's not documented, it didn't happen.

This is something you're going to hear a lot in medical school, and for good reason. Medical notes are legal documents, no matter how bad the handwriting, and form pretty much the entire source of evidence in any court case where patient care is put under scrutiny. So as you can imagine, the advice given to all brand new medical students and doctors is as follows:

Document everything. *Everything.*

If you do or say anything to a patient, relative or colleague, be sure to jot it in their notes so that the rest of the medical team know. It doesn't have to be an essay and it doesn't need to be particularly well written; the only requirement is that another member of the medical team can understand what happened and what the outcomes are without needing to ask you for information. You wouldn't believe the number of *'oh I'd already done that…'s* that happen on the ward purely because people hadn't documented it in the notes. It's not just time that gets wasted either, money gets spent on repeated forms, samples, tests, and it can even lead to patient harm if they have a second, unnecessary blood test or X-ray because the first one got forgotten about.

So whatever you do, *document or die!*

As for actually doing the documenting, learning to write in the notes can seem rather daunting when you're a medical student, as all the doctors seem to know what to write and as a med student you don't want to mess up these very important notes. Well I'll let you in on a little secret; if you write something in the notes that is:

▶ true

▶ legible

▶ at least a bit relevant to that particular patient,

then you have contributed legitimately and helpfully to the cause. The worst that can happen is someone ignores what you've written, and if you watch any senior doctor heaving through the vast stack of notes you'll realise most of the time they're ignoring half of it anyway. In fact what you actually find often happens is that a medical student has spent more time talking with the patient than any of the doctors, notices something that was previously missed, such as a previous problem with certain medications or relevant piece of family history, and their documentation then has a bearing on that patient's future care, so don't for a second think that you shouldn't be writing in the notes. Get used to doing it, learn the lingo that the team likes to use, and start leaving your mark on the world!

Paediatrics

AND WHAT DID YOU FIND ON EXAMINATION?

...I'M TERRIFIED OF BABIES.

THE GREEN COLOUR OF THE DISCHARGE FROM THIS CHILD'S EAR WOULD SUGGEST PSEUDOMONAS INFECTION

GOOD. HOWEVER THE GREEN CRAYON IN HIS HAND WOULD SUGGEST OTHERWISE

unicyclemedic

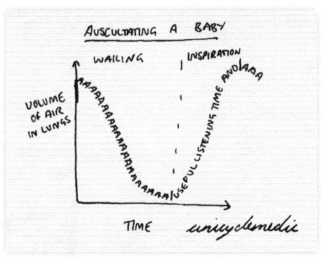

AUSCULTATING A BABY

WAILING   INSPIRATION

VOLUME OF AIR IN LUNGS

AAAAAAAAAAAAAAAAAAAAAAA/USEFUL LISTENING TIME AND/AAA

TIME   unicyclemedic

PATIENT IS UNEMPLOYED, DOESN'T DRINK OR SMOKE AND DOESN'T DRIVE...

I'M GUESSING YOU'RE NEW TO PAEDIATRICS?

AND IS SHE PRODUCING WET NAPPIES?

SHE HASN'T IN A WH.. NOPE, THERE IT IS.

unicyclemedic

Nappies are like baby-barometers. If they're producing lots of not-too-stinky urine, then everything is *probably fine*.

Babies don't like stethoscopes. They're scary and cold and rarely fluffy. To get around this problem I hand it to the child the second they walk in the room and say, *"Hey, what's this?"*, and let them play with it while I talk to Mum / Dad. When it comes to listening time, I ask the child if I can borrow the earphones and then show them how I listen to the parent's chest (always be smiling). Then offer it to the child; *"would you like to have a go?"*. Doesn't always work, but often it's enough for them to keep quiet while you listen. If you can't settle a child and they're crying relentlessly, just wait until that momentary inspiration between wailing that tells you if the lungs are clear.

Demonstration of the Moro reflex is a curious spectacle. The aim is to give the baby the sensation of falling, to see if its arms automatically try to grab onto something, presumably a vestigial survival tool from when we lived in trees. In reality the more reliable response is the mother shrieking as her precious newborn is essentially dropped on purpose with a thud. The baby is not harmed, but often cries, and as such it is imperative that you prepare the parents beforehand.

"I'm about to test a reflex called the Moro reflex. I gently let baby flop back onto the bed and see if he grasps with his hands to stop his fall. He will probably cry because it's a little scary for him, but I promise you it won't harm him."

One doctor I shadowed would prepare all parents in this way, and every time they thanked him and were interested to see the reflex in action. Another doctor did not, and received several complaints and even a threat to sue for 'throwing my baby'.

You have been warned.

Neurology

Pro tip: 💡

When sitting trying to learn something for an exam that you will probably never use, picture yourself standing on ward round in front of all your friends and one very angry consultant in front of you. The consultant has asked you a question about the topic in front of you – would you know what to say?

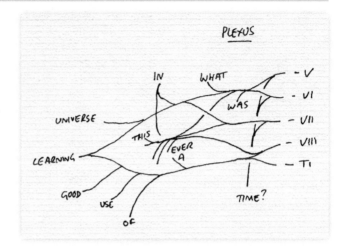

Everything you need to know for neurology is as follows:

1. If you test tone, power, reflexes, coordination, proprioception and sensation then you can't be shouted at for doing a bad examination.

2. In general, the more stuff that is affected, the higher up the lesion.

If they can't feel their toes, but everything else is fine, the problem is probably the nerves in the foot. If they have a weakness affecting all of one side of their body, the problem is in the brain. Simple.

Headaches are usually not caused by something serious, except for when they are.

Going to theatre

Going to theatre and scrubbing in is a great bit of medical school, even if you're not particularly surgically-minded. You get to dress up like they do in the TV shows that you won't admit were the real reason you applied for medicine, and then observe and even assist in gory procedures that would see you end up in prison for a very long time if you didn't have a medical degree.

Spending time in theatre is much like medical school as a whole, in that the more you put into it, the more you'll gain. If you stand quietly in the corner, unable to

SUCTION DUTY.

MILDLY BETTER THAN
BEING RETRACTORMAN.

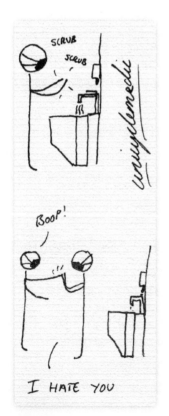

I HATE YOU

see anything interesting and don't ask any questions, I promise you they'll forget you're even there. It was crazy the number of times I've heard my colleagues at med school saying things like,

"I went to theatre for a bit, but they didn't get me to do anything and it wasn't useful so I left".

The whole point is that the onus is on *you* to get as much out of it as possible. Make sure you ask for stuff. Be bold! Ask to scrub in, or be shown how to. Ask to stand a bit closer so you can see the good stuff. Question the surgeons on what the slimy red bit next to the slimy white bit is. Ask why they're using that tool for that bit of the operation. Surgeons love talking about their work, and most of them love teaching. Just remember that they're concentrating on the operation in front of them so it's hard to think of stuff to ask a medical student who's hiding in the corner. Imagine someone puts a more junior student in front of you and says, *"teach them something."* It takes a lot of effort to think of stuff on the spot to teach. It's much easier for the surgeon to answer your questions while they get on with the job, and since they'll see that you're interested, they'll be much more likely to get you involved in the cool stuff.

Scrubbing in is scary. There's a meticulous soapy ritual that you have to follow, and then for the following few hours you have to be unnaturally aware of where your hands are to ensure that you're not about to insert a whole host of deadly bacteria into a patient's previously clean insides. As with everything in medicine, the only way to get good at scrubbing in is to do it over and over again until your muscles remember what it feels like. Watch how the surgeons and scrub nurse do it, and make sure you ask to be shown how to do it. They might say that there isn't time on this occasion but they will definitely want to teach you, so keep asking.

Once you're scrubbed in, there is one very simple rule: don't touch anything that isn't sterile. That means not touching anything that isn't blue or patient. When you're not doing anything, get into the habit of standing with your hands clasped together at the level of your xiphisternum, to stop them wandering off. If you're able to get close enough, stand right up against the operating table with your hands resting on the sterile field. You'll see more and won't accidentally scratch your head and have to go and rescrub.

This next bit is very important. You **will** mess up. You will touch something unsterile by accident, and you'll feel terrible. In a busy operating theatre, someone else may or may not notice. You **must** be honest; if you have messed up and touched something non-sterile, nobody is going to be mad at you. Everyone has done it several times, we're all human. Absolutely **do not** assume nobody saw and that it'll probably be fine, because it puts the patient at risk, and if someone *did* notice, they'll label you as dangerous, which is not something you want on your record. Just calmly step back, announce that you're not sterile any more, and go and re-scrub. Consider it useful extra practice.

Pro tip:

How long should you scrub your hands for? The answer is five seconds longer than your senior.

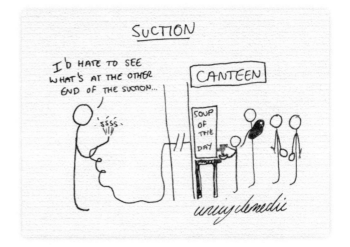

Take a look at the suction setup in theatre and you'll see the pink goop schlorping along the quivering plastic tubing to a series of pots that have measuring lines up the side. The goop collects in these pots, and the tubing then continues, goop-free, to the wall, where the negative pressure is generated. It turns out those pots are somewhat crucial, as I discovered when a colleague told me about the time her father, who helped install some of the first suction systems, was asked to deal with a 'smell' in theatres on a particularly warm summer evening. Upon lifting the ceiling access panel he was somewhat dismayed to find approximately eight inches of what can only be described as 'human soup' sitting above the ceiling of the theatre. Clearly someone hadn't realised the pots form a crucial part of the circuit, and had looked on as the stream of medical waste disappeared merrily into the wall.

Drugs

You'll have to learn some stuff about some drugs for your exams. In reality on the ward you can just download the BNF app on your phone and look it up each time, or ask one of the pharmacists, but it's helpful to know at least what *kind* of medication you're looking for, and the common side-effects. After all, you're supposed to be a doctor.

Pro tip:

Focus on emergency drugs, doses and how they're given, because you won't have time to look it up in a real emergency.

▸ *Adrenaline – 0.5mg for anaphylaxis, 1mg for arrest*

▸ *(Child under 12 is 0.3mg for anaphylaxis)*

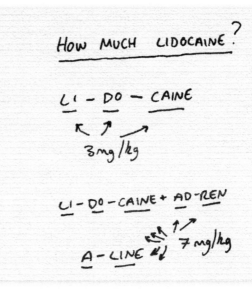

When injecting lidocaine as a local anaesthetic, it's rather important not to give too much, what with the whole makes-nerves-stop-working aspect of its pharmacological profile. So how much to give? You can give 3mg/kg of lidocaine on its own, but if you give it with adrenaline, the vasoconstriction prevents systemic spread, so you can give more.

▶ Li-do-caine = 3 syllables = 3mg/kg

▶ Li-do-caine-ad-ren-a-line=7 syllables = 7mg/kg

Naloxone

I pulled a pair of examination gloves onto my sweating hands as the paramedics wheeled the dishevelled, unconscious, urine-soaked man in his thirties into the resuscitation bay. As the nurses set about unpacking him, the Emergency Department registrar downed the last of her coffee and sauntered over to greet the team.

"Hello, my name is Michelle, I'm the ED registrar. What have we got?"

The paramedic began his spiel. *"Thirty-five-year-old male found unresponsive outside Morrison's with a history of intravenous drug use and alcohol excess. Unknown other medical history, no fixed abode. Remained unresponsive in the field, pinpoint pupils and respiratory rate of six. Two shots of naloxone 400 microgram given in the ambulance and his respiratory rate is now fifteen."*

The man remained motionless but was groaning loudly as the nurses and I began undressing him and applying the ECG electrodes and blood pressure cuff. As we went to slide down his damp and somehow simultaneously crispy trousers the registrar jumped in,

"Watch out for his pockets."

I froze. What on earth does that mean? As it turns out, a lot of needle users load themselves up and then simply pop their sharps back in their pocket for next time, and if you go near their pockets there's a fair-to-middling chance you get stuck with a very dirty, drug- and blood-laden needle. Wise words indeed. I looked at my hands to see if I was already bleeding. All good.

We finally got his trousers off and a gown on, and established intravenous access before giving another shot of naloxone. I asked the registrar,

"How long does it take for the naloxone to wor…"

"YAAAAAAAAAAAARGH!!!!!!" the man sat bolt upright, almost headbutting one of the poor nurses in the process, sweat pouring down his face, his maddened eyes darting around the room, searching for the culprit who had dragged him mercilessly down from his near-fatal high.

"Not too long," she replied dryly, *"so make sure you've got your cannulas in before you wake them up"*.

It's useful to learn some of the antidotes for common toxins, or drug overdoses, with naloxone as the antidote for morphine or heroin overdose always a popular question. Just remember that naloxone has a very short half-life, so it may well wear off twenty minutes after you've given it, and the patient goes unresponsive again. This is fine in hospital where you can keep an eye on your patients, but it means you have to be careful with heroin users in A&E. On more than one occasion they've received the naloxone and woken up, before absconding and running out onto the street (with a convenient new cannula in their arm) only to be found collapsed ten minutes later.

Probably the most high-yield antidote fact as far as exams go is knowing the antidote for paracetamol overdose is NAC or N-acetylcysteine. Your liver has a limited capacity to break down paracetamol by sticking sulphur groups on it, and once you've exceeded that capacity it spills over into a different metabolic pathway that produces NAPQI, the toxic byproduct that wrecks your liver, among other things. To solve this problem you need to give the patient vast quantities of sulphur to help speed the healthy pathway and avoid the nasty one. Because trying to take oral sulphur is like drinking liquid fart, we give intravenous NAC instead. There's a special graph to decide whether you watch and wait or treat the patient, as there is a small risk of anaphylaxis with giving NAC unnecessarily; however, if there is any doubt over the time course of the overdose then you must treat.

WHAT IS THE TREATMENT FOR N-ACETYL CYSTEINE OVERDOSE?

...PARACETAMOL?

Pro tip: 💡

Many drugs don't have an antidote, so the go-to answer is "supportive treatment".

Side effects

Memorising a few of the common side effects of drugs will help you out with your history-taking, especially if you can't find an explanation for someone's symptoms. Lots of drugs cause diarrhoea and nausea (and people will often say they're *allergic* as a result), and it's important to elicit how severe any side effects are, as it's a common reason that people stop taking their medications. Asking, *"how do you get on with your medications?"* is often a useful question, as patients may say,

"I stopped taking my ramipril years ago because it made me cough so much and my amlodipine made my ankles swell, but I didn't want to bother my GP because I know she's busy."

And now you have a reason for why their blood pressure is through the roof.

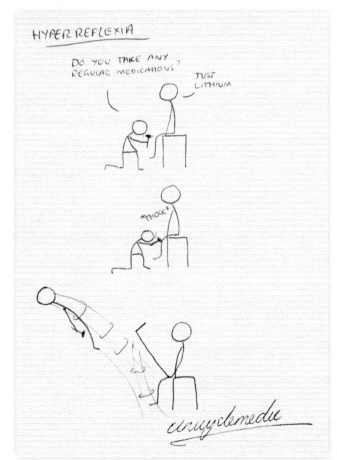

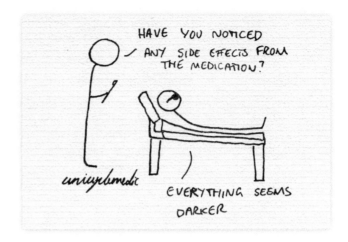

There are side effects, and then there are 'side effects'.

Pro tip: 💡

It's good to know the evidence base behind the drug you're prescribing. You'd be surprised how many drugs are given that actually aren't all that strongly supported by the data.

Drug stories

I started writing my blog unicyclemedic.com in third year, as a collection of revision stories. I found it difficult to remember long lists of things, such as drugs causing particular side effects, and found that by making a little story up I could link them together and improve my recall. They're completely ridiculous, which actually helps as it makes them more memorable, and I've included a couple here to give you a flavour. Try it for yourself, and see if it is a technique that improves your learning!

Drugs that damage the liver

Mr Isoniazid is sitting in a café playing cards over a bottle of wine and a Guinness with his best pal Dave. Dave is on oestrogens because he wanted a pair of magnificent breasts to complement his favourite mushroom hat, and Mr Isoniazid recently bought a plastic halo that he wears above his head, but unfortunately it's giving him a headache so he took some paracetamol. He also has a UTI.

Hepatotoxic drugs:

▶ Isoniazid

▶ ACE inhibitors

▶ Alcohol

▶ Iron (Guinness used to be prescribed for its high iron content)

▶ Oestrogens

▶ Antifungals – fluconazole, ketoconazole, itraconazole

▶ Halothane

▶ Paracetamol

▶ Trimethoprim

Drugs that cause intracranial hypertension

▶ Isotretinoin

▶ Steroids

▶ Lithium

▶ Tetracyclines

▶ Levothyroxine

▶ Oral contraceptive

▶ Cimetidine

Mr Hot-Headed is a keen bodybuilder who likes to ride his ridiculous four-wheeled bike around and show off his muscles. He's recently taken to injecting steroids to improve his muscle bulk, and his friends are all terribly impressed. His girlfriend wanders up to him to say how hot and shaky she feels from her levothyroxine medication, when he notices that she's massively pregnant. This takes him by surprise, and he can't find the right words to express his feelings before his head explodes.

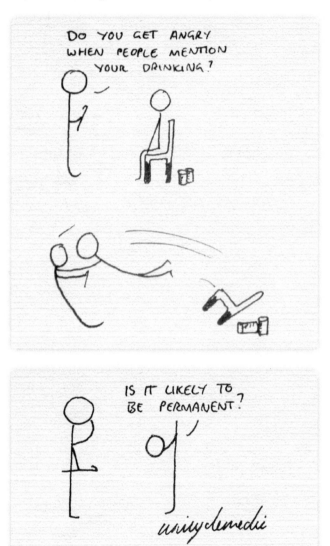

CHAPTER SIX

Doubt and being a happy student

I'm an incredibly neurotic individual. Always have been, and likely always will be. I obsessively check things and constantly criticise my own performance when I don't meet my own ridiculously high expectations, and as a result I've spent a lot of my life being incredibly sad, as persistent self-doubt slowly constricted the enjoyment out of everyday life. As a medical student, I would worry endlessly about what I would have to do that day on the wards, and whether I'd be able to do it. Maybe I'd be asked to do a difficult cannula, or have to perform a respiratory exam in front of the ward round. As a junior doctor I still panic all too frequently about whether I've missed something, or prescribed a drug incorrectly. Twice I have driven back to the hospital well after my shift had ended 'just to check' that everything was fine. Of course it was, and is, always fine, and even when I wasn't successful or things didn't go as planned, it was never as bad as I'd made it out to be.

It's not something that gets talked about all that much, especially not in high-pressure environments such as medicine, where any mention of anxiety or doubt is considered 'weakness', but it's something I've discovered a huge proportion of the general population, and especially medical students, have in common. Colleagues I've opened up to about my own worries have revealed that they too are dealing with similar issues of worrying too much, and I firmly believe that those same characteristics of wanting to be successful, to help people and to take responsibility that drive us to become doctors are the ones that also predispose us to the high rates of crushing anxiety, depression and suicide that we tragically see so much of in the world of medicine.

I've often found myself preoccupied with what other people think of me as an individual, and the baseline assumption has always been a fairly negative one. As a result I noticed effects on my concentration, losing interest in things and generally becoming less and less motivated to get stuff done, because *what's the point?* There have been huge numbers of things that I wish I had done, but never did, simply because of what others might think. It seems so strange looking back and thinking, *'what was I worried about?'* but at the time that constraining fear of embarrassment or rejection is so powerful that you can find yourself paralysed by that anxiety.

I've always enjoyed weird things like circus tricks and magic (*hence the name*), but never really pushed myself to get good or show anyone else because it was just too scary to put myself up for scrutiny by those around me. I once rode my unicycle to lectures, and it felt absolutely brilliant. But I found the whole experience was ruined by the embarrassment and fear that I'd made someone, somewhere, think I was an idiot for doing so.

Over recent years I've gradually come to the realisation that what actually makes me happy, and I mean *genuinely* content with myself and my life, has very little to do with other people at all. Even less to do with what they're thinking. To this end, I wrote down a list of the common characteristics of things that I would say *actually* make me happy as a person:

▸ *Learning new information*

▸ *Mastering new skills and improving old ones*

▶ *Making other people feel better*

▶ *Exercising*

▶ *Creating something meaningful or beautiful.*

That was it. My whole life, everything I've ever wanted and am ever going to need, is in those five bullet points. I call them my *big five*.

Imaginative, I know…

I wanted to be a doctor because I believed it would cover the first three of these, and so far it certainly has. The wealth of continually growing knowledge and development in medicine would ensure I could never possibly run out of things to learn, and the practical procedures are always great fun to practise and rewarding when they go well. Hopefully I'm making people feel better along the way as well.

To begin with, thinking about things using this simple framework seemed to work well; however, what I discovered was that no matter how hard I tried, my neurotic brain was always rather proficient at throwing a negative spin on each of these characteristics, and pretty quickly they morphed into a rather bitter, menacing set of doubts:

▶ *I'll never learn all the necessary information*

▶ *There will always be someone better than me*

▶ *I can't help everyone, and at some point I'm sure to screw up and make it worse.*

This threw me into a tailspin, and I lost considerable faith in what I was doing. Every time I attempted to do a procedure, learn new information when revising, or take a history from a patient, my self-doubt would churn away, leaving me totally disheartened and unmotivated. Something needed to change if I was to remain motivated to tackle such a demanding career, and maintain a healthy and happy lifestyle.

So I started to break things down to the level of the big five.

Is this going to teach me anything?

Is it making me better at something?

Is it helping other people?

Is it exercise?

Is it creative?

I focused entirely on these five. I tried to only do things that fulfil at least one of them, and when I *was* doing something that did, I didn't question it. Of course the acid anxiety would seep through these cracks of optimism, trickling thoughts of doubt tugging away at my motivational drive, but I forced myself to say *'yes, this is a good thing that I'm doing, and I'm going to keep going'.* It was knackering, and often I'd have to give up and try again, but eventually I got to the point where I was confident enough to do a quick mental check *'yup, this is fine',* and get on with it.

The result?

I got happy.

Not laugh out loud happy. Not even smiling happy. Just *content.* It was huge, and weirdly physically embracing – everything felt warmer and all the colours in the day somehow had a brighter hue. People seemed friendlier while day-to-day jobs seemed more enjoyable. My concentration began to improve to the point where I could sit comfortably for up to an hour and a half, gently plodding away through some work, and actually enjoy it. I found my working memory steadily improving as it was no longer clogged with negative assumptions like some stagnant oil filter, and my interest in both my work and the people with whom I interacted steadily rose too. Of course I still worry about things, that's just who I am and it makes me a better doctor when I can use it properly, but I find myself panicking a lot less about the little things that I later look back on and think,

"Why the hell was I worried about that?"

Pro tip:

If it were easy, everyone would do it. The reason medicine as a profession is held in such high regard by so many societies is because it is difficult, demanding and emotionally draining. Accepting this and allowing yourself a break now and again will give you the strength needed to get through it. No matter how slick and confident they may seem, nobody is finding it easy.

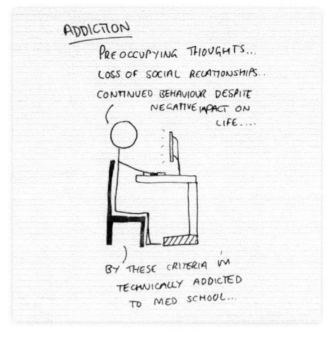

Medical school is addictive. Make sure to break the habit once in a while.

Do other stuff

The concept of having 'balance' in your life is bandied around a lot, and people widely agree that it's good to be a 'balanced' person. From an orthopaedic perspective, balance is certainly helpful for good health. From a career point of view it simply means 'not doing one thing all the time'. Try to find one or two other things that you enjoy doing outside work. It takes the pressure off and allows your brain to step off the treadmill for a while.

Pro tip: 💡

Tracheal deviation is a really late sign in tension pneumothorax. If they have rapidly worsening shortness of breath, distended neck veins, absent breath sounds and hyper-resonance on one side, whack a needle in and get an X-ray. Whether you're right or wrong, they're going to have a pneumothorax on the X-ray.

"The pleasure of a physician is little, the gratitude of patients is rare, and even rarer is material reward, but these things will never deter the student who feels the call within him."

Theodor Billroth (1829–94)

"Always do your best. What you plant now, you will harvest later."

Og Mandino

"Life is 10% what happens to you and 90% how you react to it."

Charles R. Swindoll

It's okay to fail

"If you fail, then you don't get what you want."

This concept is drilled into every student, for every exam, forever. Conceptually it makes sense that if you don't pass the exam or test, or project, then you don't get to enjoy the reward of the prize it so ominously guards; that admission to the medical school of your dreams, progression to the next academic year, or driving a car. So it came as a bit of a surprise when during my time at med school I discovered that just occasionally, failure will get you exactly what you're looking for…

I'll elaborate. Medicine, being the beautiful all-encompassing lifestyle that it is, requires not only a certain knowledge base, but also demands proficiency in a variety of practical tasks. Taking blood, suturing wounds and siting cannulas, to name just three, all require practice, and nothing can replace repetition when it comes to encoding that muscle memory that makes the registrar look so good as they breeze in and nail it first time.

Along the way, you're not expected to get it right every time, clearly. As a beginner you are expected to make mistakes, and all that can be asked of you is that you put your best effort into your work, and try to learn from it, when it goes wrong. I knew this as much as the next person; however, being the neurotic perfectionist that many med students are, I was still overwhelmed with anger and frustration every time I didn't succeed. I began to dread performing these procedures, as each occasion to try was another opportunity to fail, another chance to fall back into that well of pathetic *'why can't I do this?'* despair. After all, it was so much easier just to let someone else do it…

Then one day, having summoned the courage to attempt siting a cannula, I failed yet again. And again. That familiar thick cloud of self-loathing and anger began to crawl up my spine as I begrudgingly asked the doctor to take over once more. He smiled; *"Sure."* He promptly then took three attempts himself before calling the anaesthetist to come and help. *"Shit veins,"* he chirped, before heading off to do something else. I was amazed. There wasn't a shred of disappointment or frustration as he wandered away, the fact that he hadn't succeeded clearly wasn't a problem; it was beyond his ability and he needed some help. The anaesthetist took three attempts herself before that tiny plastic tube yielded any blood, and she explained to me how best to hold down the skin so as to keep the vein from wriggling away as you dive for it. She then smiled and said *"well done for having a go!"* and disappeared to go and be awesome somewhere else.

For the first time I had failed and simultaneously realised it's totally okay. That's the whole point of having a team, so that one person can help another out when they're having trouble. Since then, I've never been scared to at least have a go at something, knowing that there's a troop of supportive team members behind me should I need them. Because I tried, and had the opportunity to fail, I now know the best way to hold the skin to stop the vein wriggling away (use the thumb of your non-needle hand to press and drag the skin towards you). I was only shown once, but years later I can still picture exactly in my head how the consultant did it – why? Because I was so frustrated, so emotionally invested in the situation that it was burned into my memory forever. It's the same every time I get something wrong – I always remember perfectly what the doctor or nurse correcting me says, because of that pure emotional attention that you only pay when you're upset. So from now on, I relish the opportunity to have a go, and to fail, because I know I'm going to learn something, and remember it forever.

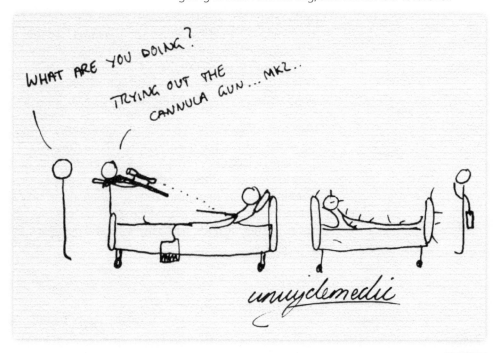

"Imagine that all through medical school you are carrying a bucket. A big bucket. And it's full of stupid. Your job is to swing that bucket around and try to spill all that stupid before you qualify."

A rather strange way of saying 'make mistakes, and make them at med school while you're not responsible!'.

Needlestick

"Tourniquet. Cleany wipe. Safety needle. Blood bottles. Cotton wool. Tape. Gloves. Good."

I sauntered confidently over to the little old lady lying in the bed at the end of the surgical ward, as she lay curled up in the sheets hiding from the world. Introducing myself, I explained that I had come to take some blood, and I washed my hands. My fifth set of bloods that morning; the doctor I was shadowing that week had already thanked me for helping reduce the workload on the morning round and for once I was starting to feel like a useful member of the team.

"She's very difficult to bleed, I can help hold her arm if you like, because she flinches a lot," the student nurse kindly offered. I gratefully accepted and as she reassured the poor lady, I set about looking for a vein. As I slid the needle in, the lady flinched, the student nurse valiantly holding onto her arm, but the needle stayed true and that familiar feeling of joy appeared as the flashback of blood snaked its way down the tube.

Moments later it screeched to a halt, tantalisingly close to the bottle. I pulled the needle back a little in case I was up against a valve, but no success, so I found my cotton wool in order to pull the needle out and try again. At this point the lady flinched again, and my right hand swing just close enough to my left to let me feel the electric flick of the needle darting into my wrist, and out again, as if nothing.

No.

That did not just happen.

I looked at my wrist as that ugly pearlescent globe of blood gradually ballooned out of my skin, confirming my fears. At first I wouldn't believe it. I couldn't have, I'm so careful! I've done this so many times without a problem. Not me; I had done all the online modules about safe venepuncture and got full marks. The needles are virtually idiot-proof; how had this happened?

A surge of anger broiling with fear burst over me, sweat rolling down my back and my throat welling up. I wanted to scream. I hurriedly tidied up the equipment and ran off to the nearest sink. The glove now had a film of blood smeared around its inner layer, mocking the futility of my situation.

Encourage the wound to bleed.

I stood there for what seemed like an hour with my hand under the hot tap, watching the thin trail of blood run off my wrist into the sink, imagining millions of viruses pouring down the drain, praying they'd all be flushed out of my system. My mind went blank.

Shit.

Shit shit shit shit shit.

HIV, Hep B, CMV, EBV... all the possibilities ran through my head. *How likely is it that she has HIV? Did I read it in her notes? How likely is transmission? What about the fact that I was wearing gloves? The wound bled straight away – that's good... Shit.*

I'd done everything right, that's what hurt the most. I'd done nothing wrong, it was just an unfortunate timing issue. I spent the rest of the afternoon in a daze as I plodded off to occupational health to be told just how likely it is that I've now got a life-changing virus, before heading back to my seniors to explain. She was a 'very low risk' patient apparently, with no history of blood-borne viruses, which is nice.

What surprised me was everyone's reaction, as if I'd got a parking ticket because I'd missed the payment limit by two minutes. It was one of those annoyances that happens more often than it should, not some extreme failure on my part that I'd thought it was. People were actually sympathetic, and recounted times when they had done the same thing, and had exactly the same feelings of panic and despair. I gradually came round to the idea that I was actually incredibly lucky. I've taken blood many times from people with very nasty viruses that would have presented a much greater risk to my health, but it happened to me on this patient, a 'very low risk' one. Thank heavens. I got a free hepatitis B booster that I was overdue for anyway and the lovely OH nurse demonstrated rather patronisingly on me how not to needlestick oneself, as she took my own blood for testing later.

One day, three needles, and I was on the business end of all of them.

As I got home I put my bag down and shuffled into the kitchen in a bewildered search for food, flustered by the day's events. I promptly stubbed my toe on the fridge door and then proceeded to burn my thumb on the frying pan.

Sigh. Let's try again tomorrow.

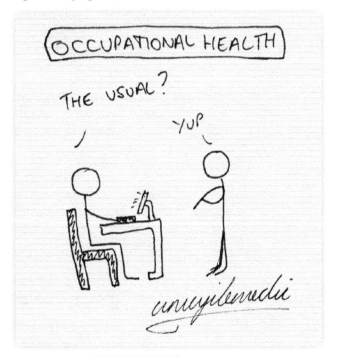

Don't be afraid to look around

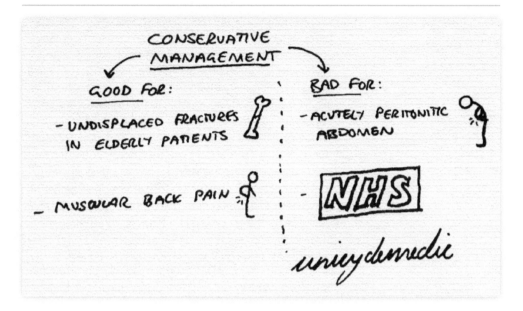

The NHS is a pretty turbulent place right now, and has been for a while. In itself it is an incredible achievement of humanity and a wonderful reflection of what civilisation can do when it bands together to try to do some good. However, it's very difficult to run such an enormous, ungainly behemoth of an institution, especially when its funding is decreasing dramatically and the workload perpetually rising. As a result, the frontline staff – the nurses, doctors, paramedics and all the other workers on the shop floor – are forced to grind through to pick up the slack, and it is incredibly hard work. It is often beautifully rewarding, and when you look at your colleagues and know that despite the adversity, you all pitched in and made it happen, it does feel very good indeed. But I must emphasise – it is *very* hard work.

It is easy to settle into the mindset that because you've dedicated yourself to training to do medicine, you are therefore destined to follow that path, and any deviation from that pre-assigned route is somehow a form of failure or selling-out. It is not.

You don't owe anyone anything. You have chosen medicine, hopefully, because it interests you and as a career is likely to fulfil you in ways other professions cannot. If it does, and for a lot of people it truly does, then wonderful, carry on. However, an increasing number of people are feeling like the job they're doing is not what they signed up for, doesn't make them feel valued or fulfilled, or even makes them feel bad, as the severe limitation on time and resources means they can't provide their patients with the standard of care they'd like to. It is perfectly acceptable to feel this way, and it's important to consider whether an alternative career path would suit you better. Have a look around, try other things. If they don't attract you then great, you're in the right career already, and you'll be better off for knowing that the grass isn't greener on the other side. However, if you do like something else more, then maybe it's time to decide whether you would be happier and more fulfilled elsewhere. The one thing that you must avoid is pushing through a medical career that you hate, that leaves you drained and demoralised, on the misguided premise that you don't want to 'sell out'. Not only will you not be a happy and healthy person (the most important thing) but you will not be able to provide the compassionate care that you envisioned when you applied to medical school. There's no harm in looking.

Sometimes you can only do your best.

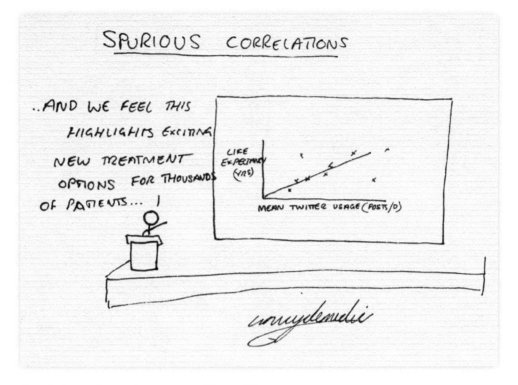

Correlation and causation are very different things.

CHAPTER SEVEN:

Studying

No medical advice book would be complete without a mention of studying. Yes, it's important to experience life on the wards and get an idea of what it is you've signed yourself up for, but at the end of the day, there are written exams to pass, and you're going to need to put in some serious book work to get through them.

The memory bucket

A quick meander through any medical school library and you'll realise that everyone studies differently. Some sit and read their way through textbooks, others write everything out on flashcards, and some insist that highlighting everything in sight is a valuable use of time. It's a personal routine that can only be decided on through experience. Having intercalated in a psychology degree, with a focus on learning about how we think memory works, I picture memory in the form of a big bucket, with a little hole in the bottom. Your brain 'experiences' information, through sight, sound (and if you're ever on the wards, smell) and generates a memory of that experience. This memory then plops into the bucket of stored information to be retrieved later on, with the most recent ones at the top. Over time these memories slowly sink to the bottom, and eventually, drop out of the little hole. Simple.

"I'll never forget the time I crashed my car…"

Ever wonder why there are some things you never forget after the first time you experience them? How is it that some memories are *just there* and you never had to consciously revise them?

Some memories are intrinsically more 'buoyant' than others, depending on how important or useful your brain deems them to be, and those memories that remain permanently at the top are your 'knowledge' – things you just *know*. Particularly emotional or frightening experiences are awarded much greater importance, and as a result often need only be experienced once for them to be scarred into your consciousness forever. Thus they float happily at the top of the bucket where they can very easily be retrieved. Meanwhile the more mundane and banal memories (medical facts included) are gradually allowed to sink over time as they don't confer such an advantage to everyday life. In order to prevent losing these memories forever, your brain has a couple of tactics up its myelinated little sleeves.

1. It can fish out a memory once in a while, polish it off, admire it and then inflate it a little, before dropping it back in the bucket at the top, a little more buoyant than before. This is **spaced repetition** and it's the reason why flashcards are such a popular studying

technique, because while it is time-consuming, it works. Each time the memory sinks more slowly, until finally it has been retrieved and inflated a sufficient amount of times to earn its place floating forever on the surface, where it becomes 'knowledge'.

2. Your brain can attach a '**hook**' to the memory to make it easier to find. This hook is a single string of thought that leads you to that memory from something else. An example would be using acronyms or mnemonics to remind yourself that the word begins with the letter B, or rhymes with 'cat', to help your brain know whereabouts in the bucket to look. The more hooks you attach, the easier the memory is to find as your brain can use any one of them to fish it out. To attach another hook you can:

> Make an acronym

> Draw a diagram

> Watch a video on the material

> Listen to someone else explain it

> Create a funny story

> Basically anything that allows your brain to access the same fact from a different angle.

Pro tip: 💡

Statistically, if you spot a malignant tumour, it's more likely a metastasis from somewhere else than a primary. If you spot a metastasis in the bone, it's probably from one of:

Prostate, Thyroid, Lung, Kidney, Breast

REVERSE ACRONYM SYNDROME

USING THE ANSWERS TO TRY AND REMEMBER THE ACRONYM YOU USED TO LEARN THE ANSWERS.

I KNOW IT'S KIDNEY, THYROID, LUNG, BREAST, PROSTATE...

AHA! PARTICULAR TUMOURS LIKE KILLING BONE!

unwydemedii

MORE MEDICAL ACRONYMS

ERCP – EMERGENCY RETROGRADE
CLERKING OF PATIENT

GACO – GRAVITY ASSISTED CONCRETE
OVERDOSE (FALL FROM HEIGHT)

LOLINAD – LITTLE OLD LADY IN NO
APPARENT DISTRESS

Not all acronyms were created equal.

♪ PITUITARY DON'T
WORK LIKE IT
USED TO
BEFORE... ♫

ED SHEEHAN

Pro tip: 💡

This is how I remember Sheehan's syndrome. I came up with it because I was always getting it confused with Asherman's syndrome. Sheehan's syndrome is pituitary gland necrosis following major haemorrhage, while Asherman's syndrome is intrauterine adhesions.

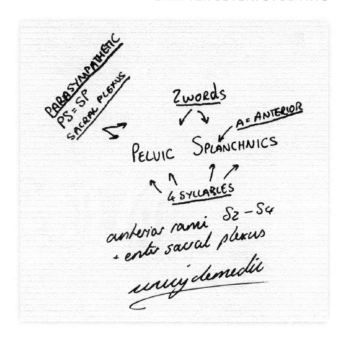

Pelvic splanchnics is two words with four syllables, (S2–S4)

The 'a' in 'splanchnics' reminds you that it's the *anterior* rami.

PS also stands for parasympathetic, and backwards is SP, reminding you they enter the sacral plexus.

As you can probably tell, I used these techniques in medical school a lot. I would listen to the lecture, go home and watch a YouTube video on the same material, listen to three or four different people explain the concept to me, create an acronym if I could, or a funny story, and then draw a picture. Usually that would give me sufficient hooks that I could retrieve the information later on without having to revise it much at all.

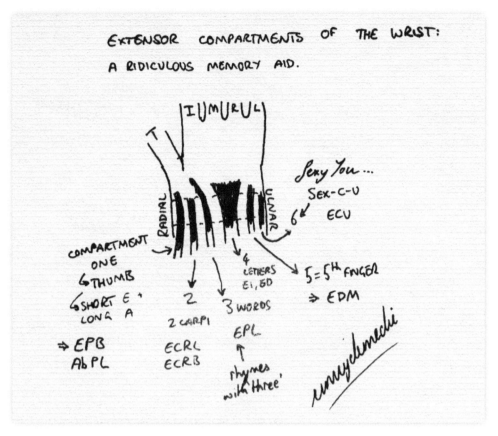

Yeah, good luck.

3. You can force your brain to assign a **greater importance** to a fact, thereby making it intrinsically more buoyant, and reducing the number of times you need to fish it out, or the number of hooks you have to attach. This is why I love getting grilled, as I mentioned earlier, because hearing why your answer was wrong, and feeling nervous and maybe a little embarrassed actually helps your brain to decide to hold on to that information for longer. Another method of increasing the importance of a fact is by doing practice questions, where you are actually **showing** your brain why you need to know that information, because it's likely to come up in the exam. Past questions also help by adding hooks to a memory, because you're approaching the answer from a different starting point using the information in the question, rather than the information in the textbook.

All three of these methods will help your brain retain and retrieve information; however, huge variety exists from person to person, and what works best for them as an individual. So this brings us back to our tour of the library, from the snacking solo scribes to the hysterical highlighters – *which way should you choose to study?*

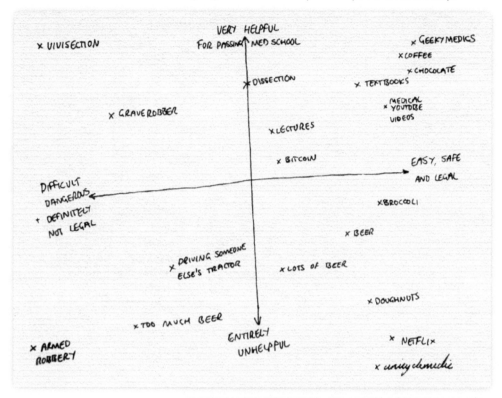

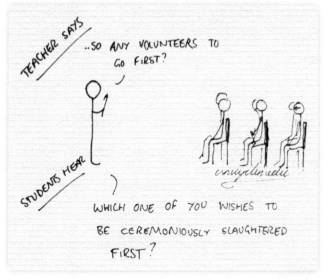

Learn how you learn

After more than fourteen years of school and six years of medicine at university, you'd think I'd have figured out for myself how I work best when it came to studying for exams. Surely after that many years of studying, cramming seemingly endless reams of information into my head for retrieval on the big day, I would know whether I was benefiting most from writing out notes, listening to lectures and podcasts, making flashcards or reading the textbooks…

I didn't.

This was a constant source of stress for me as each year I would begin the process of walking out into the lapping waters of bottomless information, and not have a clue as to how best to study. Should I try and write everything down? Type it out? Make flashcards? Just listen? Whichever tactic I tried soon became either unmanageable, tedious, or I simply didn't think I was learning anything from the process and was getting endlessly frustrated. So what did I do?

I thought about what happens when I come to **actually retrieving** the information. That is, when I'm sat in an exam and my brain is trying to dredge those answers from my big bucket of memories, and I'm cursing why I can't remember medical facts like I could with cat videos or terrible jokes, *how* is the information presented in my head? Which hooks is my brain relying on most to grab hold of those memories? Was it remembering the page of notes? Remembering the lecturer's voice? The diagram on the flashcard?

It turns out that there were predominantly four ways in which I was retrieving these facts:

▶ Remembering answers to previous questions that were similar to the one in front of me

▶ Recalling specific, often emotional experiences I'd had on the wards

▶ Diagrams that I'd drawn and re-drawn until I could do it by heart, such as the brachial plexus and anatomy of the skull base

▶ Flashcards that I'd done so many times that I didn't even have to try and remember them.

It was a very rare occasion that I would remember a piece of information from notes I'd written or textbooks I'd just sat and read. So I figured I'd stick to these four categories, and hope that my analysis wasn't way off.

How I worked for finals:

▶ I spent as much time on the wards as possible. This was largely because final year is meant to be as much of an apprenticeship as possible; you're learning how to do the job of those a year ahead of you, so you'll benefit most from observing, trying (*and failing*) to do the same things. By being on the wards, trying new things and having often frightening new experiences, I was maximising the buoyancy of those new memories and attaching as many hooks as possible!

▶ I made flashcards. This was largely a convenience thing as I could make one or two in a spare moment, and review them during quiet parts of the day. I use Anki and swear by it, as it manages your spaced repetition for you, and you have your cards with you wherever you go.

▶ Nearer the time, when exams were looming, I talked myself through a topic, while drawing out diagrams. I then used the books to check what I'd missed, and added the information to the diagram. Then I stored the diagram away until next time, and attempted to copy it perfectly. Repeat until smart.

▶ I **taught!** You never know information properly until you can teach it to someone who knows nothing about it. If you can explain something simply to a friend, parent or patient, then you can say that you truly understand a topic.

Learning is incredibly personal, and everyone does it differently. Try different methods, see which you like, and more importantly, which ones seem to *work*, and focus on those, rather than spending time doing ineffective studying that bores you and doesn't help your exam performance.

Training how you race

Having raced bikes competitively, I can say with some confidence that if you were to ask any cyclist what their 'routine' is in the run-up to a big race, you'll likely be there a while as they recount their immaculate minute-by-minute strategy to ensure optimum performance on the day. Nothing gets forgotten – food, sleep, training, clothing – you name it, a bike racer has tweaked it to beyond-neurotic perfection. So why is this of any relevance? Because I strongly believe that exams are very much like bike races. You have one day, one chance, to show the world what you can do, and you have to prepare for it to ensure it portrays you at your best. So here is my six-part plan for nailing those all-important exams at medical school!

1. Train how you race
2. Don't overdo it
3. Get your food right
4. Tapering
5. Motivation
6. The Big Day

Train how you race

There's little point in doing lots of long, gentle mountain riding if the race is a short, high-intensity blast around a velodrome. You need to train for the specific task on which you're being assessed. Likewise, if your exam is multiple choice, you'd be wise to focus on relevant practice questions rather than reading through swathes of material from a textbook. You'll start to spot the themes that get tested frequently, and there are only so many questions they can ask, so do enough, and I guarantee on exam day you'll have seen many of them before. By all means still read the information from lecture notes and textbooks, but by using MCQs to guide which areas to focus on, you'll soon figure out which information is higher yield. If, like during my first year, your exams include essay papers, then practise writing essays under timed conditions, with the same pen, in the same format, long in advance of the exam. You'll be amazed how quickly your hand gets tired, how much you improve with a little practice, and how much more confident you feel walking into the exam room.

Don't overdo it

Every competitive cyclist has overtrained. The sport is great fun, addictive, and it's easy to assume that more training means more improvement. However, the gains in your performance happen when you're resting, allowing your muscles to recuperate and rebuild. The same applies to revision; the actual learning occurs during your downtime when you're asleep, as your hippocampus (*contentious*) sifts gently through the bucket, deciding what to keep and what can be left to sink. Put the pen down, get some exercise – enough to make you slightly out of breath, and have a good night's sleep. You'll retain so much more than cramming.

Get your food right

If you try to win a race on KFC and doughnuts you will be sorely disappointed, and probably rather ill. Equally, if you're running your poor brain at max capacity for the month before your exam, and aren't fuelling it properly, it will burn out rapidly. That motivational tub of chocolate mini-bites on the desk while you study may feel like a 'lift' every time you have one, but it's doing your concentration, memory and general health no favours in the long run. Fill up on colourful, organic veg, the right kind of fats and proper protein and your performance will speak for itself. It may not seem like you have time for a 'proper' meal in exam term, but I promise that you do. Not only will the nutritional benefits improve your studying and memory, but the time spent chopping garlic is time that your brain can relax a little, consolidate the material you've just been covering and refresh itself.

I SOLEMNLY SWEAR TO GIVE OTHERS DIETARY ADVICE WHILST THRIVING ON A DIET CONSISTING ENTIRELY OF KFC AND GIN.

THE HYPOCRITIC OATH

Now, let's talk about coffee.

Caffeine has been proven to be a powerful mental and physical performance enhancer, and it works better in some people than others. If you're a java lover, work out how much is right for you well in advance of the exam, and stick to it. The key is to hit that sweet spot of concentration without getting agitated or jittery. The mistake most people make is ramping up their caffeine intake in exam term to allow them to study for longer. If you feel tired on your usual coffee fix, it means you need more sleep, not more caffeine. As counterintuitive as it may sound, you will gain more from that well-needed sleep than an extra hour's cramming. Listen to your brain and oblige.

Ever wondered how insane it is that you can encounter a smell, and immediately think, 'that's the smell of Grandma's house'? Google 'state-dependent learning'. It's awesome. Smell is linked very strongly with memory. My best guess as to why, would be that it made evolutionary sense to remember good smells and bad smells to avoid poisonous and predatory things, but who knows.

Tapering

In the weeks running up to a big event, any cyclist worth her salt will taper her training load down, to maintain her fitness while ensuring she's as fresh as possible before the race. The same goes for revision; you don't want to be cramming until five in the morning and then turning up to sit the paper demoralised and exhausted. It's the mental equivalent of running from your house to the start of a marathon! I usually work fairly solidly up until two days to go, and the day before I take it easy. I do some solid exercise, and a bit of light reading, but definitely not cramming. You want your brain to be at its absolute peak performance on the day that matters. It's hard to do, especially when you see other students outside the exam room with their heads in their books with ten minutes to go, but try to remember this: given how vast the array of topics in medicine, exactly **how** likely is it that the one thing you chose to cram on the morning of the exam will actually come up? It's much more probable that the stress causes you to lose concentration and make silly mistakes, especially late on in a two- or three-hour exam. Have faith in your method, and stay strong!

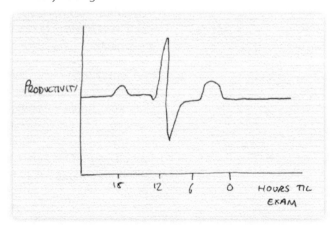

Motivation

It is really hard to stay motivated when revising, especially for insane medical exams with their endless quantities of information and undefined syllabus.

Keeping motivation up is key to productive work, as your brain remembers stuff it wants to know much better (song lyrics, cat videos, funny pictures...). When I really can't be bothered and just want to give up, I do a couple of things.

▸ Put the pen down, stop working and go make a hot drink, as there's no way that trying to push through the wall of boredom is going to do any good.

▸ While the kettle is boiling do some star jumps, lunges, press-ups, sit-ups, stretches – anything to get blood moving around the body.

The Big Day

It's showtime! A student's exam day routine is like their underwear – intensely personal, largely hidden to other students, and rarely shared with anyone else. Find what works for you and stick to it, no matter how confident and perfect the other students look. As I mentioned earlier, I make a point of doing zero work on the morning of the exam. I know that my brain struggles to concentrate for the entirety of the exam, so there's no way I'm going to work it any harder than that. Headphones on, coffee in hand, and calmly saunter past the studying / bragging / panicking / crying / smoking students outside the exam hall. Deep breath. You got this.

RTFQ

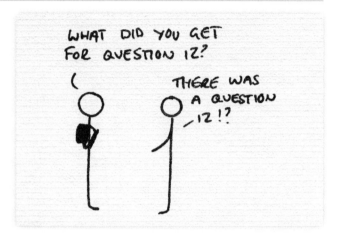

Read the full question. Printing exam papers is expensive, so every single word in every single question is there for a reason. Make sure you have read and understood every part of the question, and decided in your own mind why it is that the examiner decided to include it in the question, because I promise you *it's there for a reason*.

For example: *A 48-year-old lady from sub-Saharan Africa presents with…*

Think about what diseases affect 48-year-old ladies, and what issues occur more frequently in sub-Saharan Africa than in the UK or Europe, such as tuberculosis or malaria.

Chill out, read the whole question.

Allow yourself to celebrate

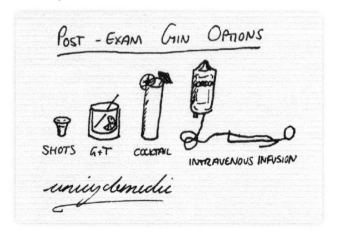

After the exam, there is nothing left to do but de-stress and celebrate. Celebrate for doing well, celebrate for it being over, celebrate for no more exams, just celebrate and be happy. You've earned it. Don't be that guy who wants to go through every question and compare answers. Nobody likes that guy.

It's very important to allow yourself to wind down after exams, however well or badly you think they went. Find something you like to do, that relaxes you, and go do it until you feel happy. You've earned it.

Q. WHICH OF THE FOLLOWING IS THE <u>MOST</u> CORRECT?

A. PERFECTLY GOOD ANSWER

B. COMPLETELY IRRELEVANT STATEMENT

C. PERFECTLY GOOD ANSWER

D. PERFECTLY GOOD ANSWER

E. NEVER SEEN THIS WORD BEFORE

unwyclemedii

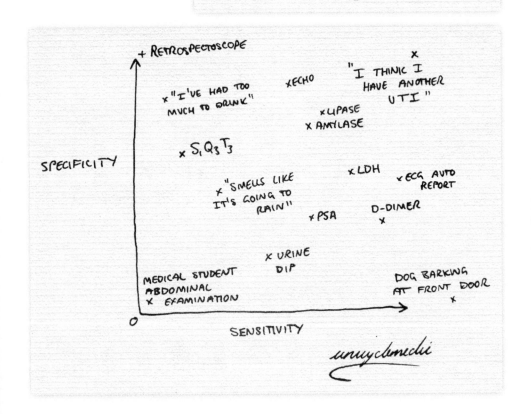

OSCEs

OSCE

WELCOME TO YOUR EXAM.
THERE ARE TWELVE STATIONS TO
COMPLETE. YOU CHOOSE THE ORDER
BASED ON HOW SICK YOU FEEL
THE PATIENT IS. AT FORTY
MINUTES, NINE MORE WILL BE
ADDED.
YOU WILL ALL TAKE 20mg
FUROSEMIDE BEFORE YOU BEGIN.

ANY QUESTIONS?

OSCEs, or to use their proper name *objective structured clinical examinations*, are rather interesting beasts. They represent a valiant attempt by the medical education system to take the impossibly random, chaotic world of clinical interactions and make them structured and remotely measurable, and to be fair, for the most part they're pretty successful. Actors and patient educators are hauled in every year to cry, scream, shout and wince hundreds of time over in front of incredibly nervous students while a thoroughly bored examiner realises the remuneration they are receiving for their services was definitely not worth the hassle. From personal experience I have found they are terrifying whilst simultaneously being quite good fun, and without fail have always ended up learning as much from doing the exam itself as I did revising for it in the first place. There are hundreds of books that will tell you how to do well in OSCEs, so here I've just outlined the best advice I've received over the years, as well as my top tips that you might not find elsewhere.

Burn, baby, burn

I get nervous before exams. I've been told that's normal. One thing that happens before OSCEs is my hands get really cold and clammy. I then notice this, realise that it means I'm nervous, and get even more stressed out. I then go to shake a patient's hand or feel their abdomen, and it's unpleasant for them and shows them that I'm nervous as well, probably impacting on my overall score in the exam. So I started a routine of finding a sink five or ten minutes beforehand and running my hands and wrists under the hottest water I can bear for about two minutes. It makes them go bright red, forcing them to vasodilate as well as warming them up directly. They then feel warmer to me and the patient, and I have one thing less to worry about. It might not make much of a difference come station twelve, but it chills me out knowing my hands aren't freezing cold as I walk into the exam.

Dry your hands

Exam day. You've prepared. You're ready (ish). You amble confidently into the cubicle ready to whip in a cannula or thread a catheter like a clinical ninja, and wash your hands like the soap wizard that we all know you are. You then spend the next 1 minute and 47 seconds of your allocated time attempting to balloon-animal your wet hands into a pair of gloves that are just a tad too small for you. You panic. You sweat. The ballooning becomes more desperate.

Nightmare.

Spend a few seconds making sure your hands are *super* dry after washing them, and those gloves will slide right on. You can use this drying time to introduce yourself, explain the procedure and ask if the patient has any questions before you begin. The same principle applies to hand gel – take a tiny squirt of gel, and you won't be stood there smearing goop over your hands for two minutes while the patient and examiner stare at you.

Bad stations

Stations will go wrong. Sometimes it just won't go your way, it will feel terrible and make you want to run home and cry. This is normal, I promise. The important thing is *how you react*. One or two bad stations is unlikely to make you fail, but letting a bad station impact subsequent stations is commonly a reason people don't pass. It's really hard, especially when you've worked so hard and don't feel you were able to represent yourself well, but try your best not to let a bad station affect your next one. Remember, only *you* know how badly it went, the next examiner has no idea – they are a completely blank slate. Take a deep breath, smile, and **lie**. Tell yourself you did it perfectly, that it was a flawless performance. Walk in to the next station with your chest out and head held high, and make them truly believe you **nailed** the previous station. You'd be surprised how much that body language impacts the examiner's impression of your performance.

> ### Pro tip:
>
> *During your two minutes between stations, force yourself to smile. A big cheesy grin that makes you feel like an idiot. Your mood and facial expressions are intrinsically linked via a two-way street, so forcing a fake smile will actually fool your brain into thinking you're having a better time than you are. I kid you not.*

My Communication OSCE top 5

One brand of OSCE station that comes up is 'explaining and communicating', in which one must demonstrate one's prowess in the task of bringing a patient up to speed on a condition, treatment or test result in as kind, clear and concise a way as possible. There are also 'breaking bad news' stations where you may have to inform a patient about a cancelled operation, medical mistake or terminal diagnosis. These are possibly the least realistic scenario, as on the wards it's a tad unlikely that an F1 doctor, who has been qualified for all of twenty minutes, would be given responsibility for explaining such critical information to the patient. They are, however, incredibly useful for getting you into the habit of making sure the patient understands what is going on and feels they can ask if they don't understand something, and this is important for everything from taking blood to explaining why they need another X-ray – something you definitely *will* be doing a lot as an F1.

As a general rule, the second you tell a patient any form of 'bad news', their ability to listen to what you say next goes out the window, because they begin worrying and thinking about lots of other things.

Saying *"I have some important news"* in a neutral voice with effective eye contact will usually set the tone of a difficult conversation. It signposts the patient to concentrate carefully on what you're about to say, without immediately sending them into a panic about how they're supposed to deal with this new situation.

The difficulty with explaining stations in OSCEs is that you have to ensure the patient has received enough information within the eight minutes you're given, without drowning them in a plethora of overwhelming jargon. You can't be overly reassuring when discussing test results or diagnoses, but equally you don't want to crush their spirit. So what's the secret?

Practice.

Not the answer people want to hear the night before an exam, but truly the only way to master a task this demanding is through experience, working out what

> **Pro tip:** 💡
>
> *If you say to a patient, 'I need to do a blood test', most of the time they will begrudgingly agree, because you're the doctor. If, however, you say, 'We would like to check your kidneys are working as well as they should, and to do this we would need to do a blood test', you'll often find a much more positive response. It puts them in more control, the necessity of the test is apparent and there is a direct benefit that the patient sees, rather than just another needle (or three).*

works best for you and seeing how different patients respond. No two people are the same, nor will one tactic work for everyone, so it's good to build a toolkit of techniques that you can use depending on the person in front of you. On the other hand no amount of practice is going to help if you don't have a good recipe in the first place, so here's a summary of what should be done in *any* explaining station, if you want to set off on the right track.

1. You're a doctor

Or medical student, depending on what the vignette says. That means you should employ your ethical guidelines as a medical practitioner and do your utmost to:

▶ Do no harm

> *wash your hands*

> *ensure you have the right patient!*

> *don't say anything that will unnecessarily upset your patient*

> *protect vulnerable patients (e.g. children, abused partners, very ill patients)*

▶ Respect the patient as an individual

> *give them accurate, relevant information*

> *allow them to make their own, informed decisions*

> *tell them what you would like to know if you were in their position*

▶ Do what you can to try to help the patient

> *give options for treatments, including alternatives*

> *give reassurance where appropriate*

> *provide emotional support*

> *ensure they always leave with a plan.*

As a general rule, if you do all of the above in any communication station, you'll pass the station. It won't always be simple, and the ethical principles won't always align. Sometimes you may have to *hurt* the patient (*giving bad news, venepuncture, reducing a fracture*) in order to help (*diagnosis, treatment, promoting bone healing*). Your job as a medical professional is to decide which are the most important in each situation, based on where the patient's best interests lie. Clinical judgement. Fun.

2. What do they know already?

This is my favourite bit, and is arguably the most useful for you as the time-constrained explainer. Ask the patient what they've been told so far, and what they understand, and what they say will save you huge amounts of time. By listening to their response you will then know:

▶ *at what level to pitch the information by hearing how they talk and what language they use*

▶ *what they know already, and thus what you don't need to talk about*

▶ *what bits they're most concerned about, which you can then address in more detail.*

The last one is the most important.

You may feel that it is imperative that the lady in front of you who has just had a splenectomy knows that she will be at risk of infection by encapsulated bacteria such as *Haemophilus influenzae* B, and you'd be right – it is important information. However, if her main concern is being able to go to her cousin's wedding next week, and you don't ask, then she will leave unsatisfied. Many patients will feel they can't interrupt or ask questions, and so risk leaving without having their questions answered. So ask them and ye shall find.

3. Confidentiality is key

A doctor is endowed with the huge privilege of being able to keep secrets from everyone. Patients should be able to discuss absolutely anything they like with you, their doctor, without fear of embarrassment or repercussion. There are a smattering of specific circumstances in which you are required by law to disclose information to the relevant authorities, as there may be preventable risk of harm to someone else, such as in a stabbing or shooting incident, where the police must be informed. Likewise, if you know a patient suffers from seizures and is still driving, the DVLA must be made aware. This is usually done by telling the patient they have a duty to report it, and if they don't, you will be obliged to do so. However, the vast majority of the time, you should never ever ever share anything anyone has told you outside of the medical team working on the case. So in your explaining station, think:

▶ *Does this person need to know this information?*

> *a parent always needs to know information about their newborn infant, but do they always need to know everything about their 17-year-old adolescent?*

▶ *Am I breaking confidentiality by revealing this?*

▶ *Should I conduct this conversation with/without the patient's relative/partner/friend in the room?*

4. Know your limits

Often you won't know the answer to their question, and that is totally acceptable, as you can't be expected to know everything. Don't lie, don't make something up, don't say *"I have no idea"*, but say something useful, such as:

"What I'll do is print you out a leaflet with all the information that you can take home with you."

"There is fantastic information on the NHS/Patient websites."

"I'll double-check what the current guidelines say and let you know."

I can promise you that patients will appreciate your honesty, and they definitely won't appreciate it when they realise you're making something up to try and look clever.

5. Listen

Half of the time in an OSCE you slip into a rut where you're thinking only about what you're going to say or do next. This is fine to some extent in a procedure or an examination, but in an explaining or history-taking station it's a surefire way to get stuck. The thing to remember is that the 'patient' is usually an actor who has been given a sheet of information relevant to the station. They can *only* say stuff that's on that sheet, they can't make up new facts or symptoms because then that station is no longer standardised and can't be marked objectively by the examiner. As a result, every single thing the patient says is said for a reason; there is very little room for waffle. So listen carefully to what they tell you because I can promise you, you're going to want to hear it.

Remember:

▶ *The patient / actor has been given a list of answers*

    ❯ *they have been given the important information that you need to elicit, so when they start telling you – actively listen to what they're saying!*

▶ *Thinking about what you're going to do next can actively lead you astray*

    ❯ *particularly with history stations, you might be thinking "I have to ask about this"; meanwhile the patient is telling you a symptom that completely changes your differential – listening and clarifying things they say (what type of pain / when is it worst / what does the discharge look like?) will be much more likely to provide you with your answer*

▶ *If you're stuck, ask them for help!*

    ❯ *it's a little more subtle than that, but saying something like "Is there anything else you think I should know about / Do you have any thoughts about what it might be?" can get you out of hot water.*

It is not easy. Don't put pressure on yourself by expecting to get it right every time. The reasons these OSCE stations exist is because they are a perfect 'dry run' that allows you to try without harming or upsetting a real patient. Believe me, there is nothing you can say in an OSCE that is going to harm someone for real, so use them to practise.

Stop talking

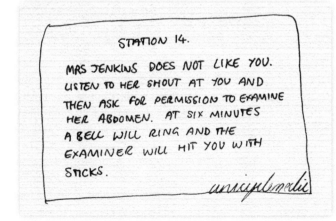

STATION 14.

MRS JENKINS DOES NOT LIKE YOU. LISTEN TO HER SHOUT AT YOU AND THEN ASK FOR PERMISSION TO EXAMINE HER ABDOMEN. AT SIX MINUTES A BELL WILL RING AND THE EXAMINER WILL HIT YOU WITH STICKS.

unsigned medic

Pro tip: 💡

Stop talking.

"The first person to speak loses" is a well-known phrase in business with regard to negotiation, and for good reason. Humans naturally find silence unsettling, especially during confrontation, and will often start talking just to fill the gaps. If you can use this tendency to your advantage, you will find that by holding your ground and staying silent, the other person will often give in and start talking. In business terms this usually means giving you more of what you want. You will not believe how powerful silence can be in an OSCE, particularly in communication stations. It's very hard to do, because the limited time available and the pressure to demonstrate your knowledge to the examiner mean you're desperate to start spewing information. But I promise you, silence is your friend when used correctly, and can mean the difference between a poorly and a brilliantly done OSCE station.

Example – without silence

"I'm very sorry, Mrs Cameron, but I'm afraid your operation has been cancelled this afternoon as there were a number of emergency trauma cases that came in unexpectedly."

"What!? How is that possible?"

"I'm very sorry, it's just that…"

"Do you know how long I've been waiting for this operation? It's despicable, that's what it is. What are you going to do about it?"

"I know it's very frustrating, and we're doing the best we can. It's just that we can't anticipate these cases…"

"Well it's not bloody good enough, I want to speak to your senior, I'm having my damned operation if it requires…"

You get the idea – lots of things have been said on both sides but not much progress made. The patient is angry, you're upset because you're only doing your best to help, and nobody is any closer to a solution.

Now try this:

Example - with judicious use of vitamin S

"I'm very sorry, Mrs Cameron, but I'm afraid your operation has been cancelled this afternoon as there were a number of emergency trauma cases that came in unexpectedly."

"What!? How is that possible?"

...silence...

"I've been waiting for months for this operation, it's ridiculous! And now I'm being cancelled again, this is just typical of the NHS. The whole system is appalling, frankly..."

...silence...

*"...Well I suppose if they're emergency cases and have to be done then they have to be done, don't they. It's just very frustrating when I haven't eaten anything all day and now I have to wait even longer. *sigh* Oh well, at least I can eat something now, I'm starving. Thank you for letting me know and sorry I got upset."*

"That's not a problem at all, can I get you a cup of tea?"

"Oh that would be lovely, thank you!"

I didn't make this up. This is a conversation I had with a lady a few months ago and it's as word for word as I can remember. What I recall most is how surprised I was at the effectiveness of keeping my mouth shut and just letting her vent, waiting out the clock as she got all of her frustrations out on the table. In the first scenario there was enough back and forth for the patient to keep getting angry, but in the second one, where there was nothing to push up against, she fizzled out and quickly came round to the idea that we were doing our best to help and was ultimately very grateful.

It was brilliant until I spilled tea over her newspaper.

ICE your patient

Ideas, concerns and expectations. This will be drilled into you at med school. *"ICE your patient"*. Make sure you have left the conversation with an idea as to what the patient feels is wrong with them (ideas), what's worrying them in particular (concerns), and what they would like done about it (expectations). After all, you're providing a service, you're not in charge of their life. Just like getting your car fixed, the mechanic's job is to work out the problem, make sure you understand it and provide options that allow you to decide what you want to do about it.

How to spot a budding neurologist

Jean-Martin Charcot was a busy chap.

Charcot's cholangitis triad is: jaundice, right upper quadrant pain, fever.

Charcot's neurologic triad (suggestive of multiple sclerosis) is: staccato speech, nystagmus, intention tremor

Charcot foot is a deformed and eroded foot that has occurred over time due to neuropathy and loss of sensation.

REFERENCE VALUES
THIS GUY KNOWS THE REFERENCE VALUES FOR EVERYTHING!
REALLY?
LEUCOCYTES..
4 – 10 × 10⁹/L
PT TIME..
11 – 15 SECONDS
COFFEE 0–9.5 /DAY
MCH 0.39 - 0.54 fmol/CELL
BREAKDOWNS
0.9 – 379.4 /MONTH
DEPENDING ON SPECIALTY
YEAH HE'S GOOD.

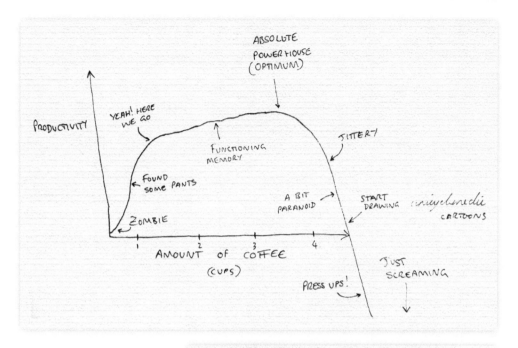

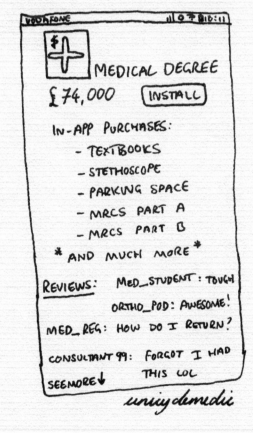

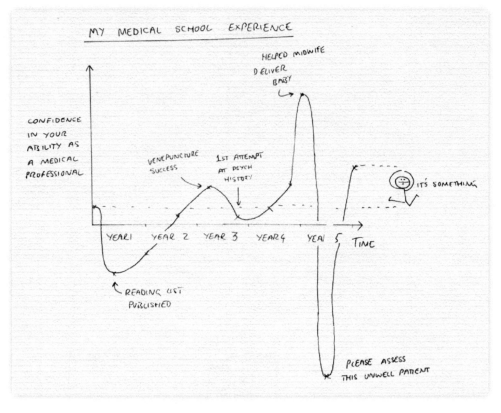

Hopefully by the end of it all, you'll feel like you have learned *something*.